PHILOSOPHY AND THE
EVOLUTION OF CONSCIOUSNESS

PHILOSOPHY AND THE EVOLUTION OF CONSCIOUSNESS

OWEN BARFIELD'S *SAVING THE APPEARANCES*

Daniel J. Smitherman

iUniversity Press

San Jose New York Lincoln Shanghai

Philosophy and the Evolution of Consciousness
Owen Barfield's *Saving the Appearances*

iUniversity Press
an imprint of iUniverse.com, Inc.

For information address:
iUniverse.com, Inc.
5220 S 16th, Ste. 200
Lincoln, NE 68512
www.iuniverse.com

ISBN: 0-595-17059-5

Printed in the United States of America

To my dad, and to Owen Barfield, who took a journey together

Epigraph

It is wisdom to cultivate the tree which you have found to bear fruit in your soul.

—Henry David Thoreau

Contents

Introduction

Barfield in Context

Forty-nine years ago, in 1951, a philosopher wrote in the preface to a new edition of his book on meaning, language, and the poetic imagination:

> It is no part of my case that push-and-pull empiricism is weak or ineffectual, only that it is, like other giants, ignorant. The possibility of man's avoiding self-destruction depends on his realizing before it is too late that what he let loose over Hiroshima, after fiddling with its exterior for three centuries like a mechanical toy, was the forces of his own unconscious mind.[i]

Six years later, the same English philosopher published a new book, in which he traced out what he called "an evolution of consciousness." The term "evolution of consciousness" must have struck many people as odd in 1957. World War II had ended a decade before. The United States government continued tests of nuclear weapons, after the first two it had developed were exploded on civilian populations in Japan. Empiricism, as positivism or scientism, exerted an influence far beyond scientific laboratories and the pages of philosophy journals.

The English philosopher was Owen Barfield, and the book was *Saving the Appearances: A Study in Idolatry*.[ii] *Saving the Appearances* was a condensation of Barfield's lifelong study of the evolution of consciousness. That lifelong study represents a profound literary effort to free the western mind from the "strait-waistcoat in which contemporary natural science has confined itself."[iii] The forty years and more since then have seen the publication of Thomas Kuhn's *The Structure of Scientific Revolutions*, widespread use of LSD, a growing interest in the work and thought of Carl Jung, and the use of the word "consciousness" as something other than what Marx called ideology. Consciousness has come to be viewed as something that one can expand, constrict, develop. There are distinct stages of development, and these stages differ qualitatively.

Intellectuals of various sorts attest to an "evolution of consciousness" and study it in detail. Some of these intellectuals suggest that the continuation and direction of this evolution lie within the influence, even the control, of individual human beings. Opinions regarding the details and nature—and even the reality—of this evolution differ, but the notion itself is a subject of discussion and study in science, philosophy, literature, and art. In spite of all this, it is arguable that we have realized that what we let loose over Hiroshima, after fiddling with its exterior for three hundred years like a mechanical toy, is the forces of our own unconscious mind.

The purpose of the following pages is to make it more clear what exactly Barfield meant by this. The way to do that, which is the working hypothesis of the book as a whole, is to place Barfield's thought as presented in *Saving the Appearances* into the context of the history of recent philosophy, from roughly 1875 to the present, in order to demonstrate the primarily philosophical character, rather than, say, the sociological or literary or historical character, of that work. There are two compelling reasons for emphasizing the philosophical character of *Saving the Appearances*:

Barfield's work is scarcely known, much less discussed, in academic philosophy, which could benefit greatly from it. Taken as a work native to philosophy, Barfield's theory of the evolution of consciousness provides special insight into the history of philosophy itself, with some very interesting results

To the degree that the contemporary mindscape of the western world, its reality principle, is fundamentally that of philosophical or logical positivism, perhaps the best angle from which to understand—and undermine—that worldview is a philosophical angle

The going gets rough at points in the following chapters, because in order to make clear what Barfield meant, and to get to a point where the sanity of his statement above is perspicuous, is palpable, the reading requires the sort of work that Barfield himself put into the task of writing. And that work, exemplified in *Saving the Appearances,* was philosophical.

It will be rewarding, though, like untying a bundle of knots in a favorite scarf or in the shoelaces of a favorite pair of shoes: we have to use our nails, and pinch hard, and look closely under a bright light. But, ah! When all the knots are loosened, and the scarf is spread out in its beautiful shimmering colors, and the laces are straightened out and evened up and the shoes pulled on and tied up snugly…All the effort has been quite worth the reward. That, I hope, is what awaits us in the pages and chapters to follow—to follow the sometimes complicated thread of an argument; to pick at the occasional Gordian knot; to unravel, in the end, a quite simple but elegant cloth of intelligibility.

I

Owen Barfield's philosophy first came into public view in the late 1920's and early 30's in England. In 1926 his book *History in English Words* was published. Two years later, in 1928, *Poetic Diction: A Study in Meaning* was published. Throughout the 1920's and 1930's he published essays and reviews,[iv] including "Milton and Metaphysics" (1923), "Metaphor" (1926), and "Thinking and Thought" (1928). In 1931 he published a review of the book *Coleridge as Philosopher*, and in 1932 published an essay entitled "The Philosophy of Samuel Taylor Coleridge." In the same year that he published his first non-fiction book, *History in English Words,* he also published the first of what would be a lifetime of contributions to journals of the Anthroposophical movement. In that year, 1926, he published "Romanticism and Anthroposophy." The two essays already mentioned, "Thinking and Thought" and "The Philosophy of Samuel Taylor Coleridge," were first published in the journal *Anthroposophy.*

Almost from the very beginning, Barfield's philosophy was involved in the thought of Rudolf Steiner, the founder of the Anthroposophical movement, and its leader until his death in 1926. Any reader acquainted with Barfield's work soon becomes aware of his debt to Steiner. From the Preface of *Poetic Diction* in 1928 to the notes in *What Coleridge Thought* in 1971, to references in personal correspondence of the 1980's, to, I am sure, the end of his long life in 1997, Barfield interjected acknowledgment of Steiner's influence and references to his work when he was not directly explicating the man's work.

To another audience, not of Barfield himself, but of his most famous friend C. S. Lewis, Barfield is a name mentioned occasionally, though always significantly. His is a shadowy presence in Lewis' early life, as Lewis attested in *Surprised by Joy.* Many fewer of Lewis' devotees know that his relationship to Barfield continued to the day Lewis died in 1963, in such a fashion that Lewis kept Barfield's book *Worlds Apart* by his bedside, along with a copy of the Bible.

A third sort of introduction to Barfield's work, which may not be over-shadowed by either Steiner or Lewis, has been for "literary people" who come to Barfield through literature and literary criticism and theory. These usually read *Poetic Diction* first, and if they go on to read other books of Barfield's, it is often *Saving the Appearances*. As Louis Mackey observed, "A lot of theologians and literary people have found the book [*Saving the Appearances*] interesting. I know a few philosophers and one political scientist who have studied it."

Which brings me to a fourth avenue of introduction to Barfield's work: philosophy. Barfield is little known, if not unknown, to most philoso-phers, judging from the lack of references to his work in mainstream and academic philosophical publications. His essay "Poetic Diction and Legal Fiction" appears in one or two anthologies of essays on the philosophy of language. Susanne K. Langer, translator and student of Ernst Cassirer, studied Barfield and observed significant parallels between Barfield's and Cassirer's thought on myth and symbolism. The philosopher Robert McDermott published an essay in 1989, entitled "Philosophy and Evolution of Consciousness,"[v] which focused on Barfield's own work as well as Barfield's interpretations and developments of Steiner's thought. And in 1992 Donna Potts published *Howard Nemerov and Objective Idealism: The Influence of Owen Barfield.*[vi] Though there are surely other reference to Barfield in regard to his philosophy proper, they cannot be many or significant, or they are simply impossible to find.

Even the references listed above are not unambiguously works of phi-losophy themselves. McDermott's essay is closest, yet it was published in an eclectic literary/spiritual/philosophical journal. Donna Potts' book is first and foremost a work of literary criticism involving considerations of philosophy. And though Langer's account of Barfield's work is positive, the few references to his "Poetic Diction and Legal Fiction" have been rhetorical and dismissive. What then is the relation of Barfield's work to philosophy?

Barfield began his schooling, writing, publishing and thinking in England of the first two decades of the twentieth century. He served in World War I, and studied literature at Oxford. His first book of non-fiction, *History in English Words,* makes occasional reference to philosophers, but he pays more and closer attention to literary figures. His second book, *Poetic Diction,* culminated his Oxford studies. He aspired to a life writing poetry and literary criticism.

Nonetheless, the atmosphere in which his work commenced and took shape also had a distinct philosophical air. Pragmatism, empiricism, logical analysis and positivism appeared and flourished during this time. Bertrand Russell (1872-1970) taught at Cambridge, and published *Principia Mathematica* in 1903.[vii] G. E. Moore (1873-1958) met Russell at Cambridge, and in the same year of 1903 published *Principia Ethica,* and the essay "The Refutation of Idealism." Ludwig Wittgenstein (1889-1951) published *Tractatus Logico-Philosophicus* in 1922. Together, these and other thinkers "fought a rebellion against idealism," and developed empiricism in the direction of logical atomism, the empirical verification of meaning, and the emotive theory of moral judgments. The cumulative nature of these impulses was an atmosphere of harsh criticism and opposition to idealism, notions of transcendent truth and meaning, religious superstitions, and aesthetic and artistic sentimentalism. Logical analysis and scientific experimentation were praised as the philosopher's most powerful and valuable tools in the work of tearing at the rotting and gaudy façade of old-fashioned philosophies.

Doris Myers suggests[viii] that an important target of this effort was the propaganda of the First World War, propaganda delivered in the terms, images and concepts of philosophical idealism. The empiricist/atomist/positivist impulse directed itself to the task of unmasking the propaganda to reveal it as empty and meaningless prattle. To this end, these philosophers brought language itself, and the English language of ethics and metaphysics, under their scrutiny, and proceeded to strip it of everything meaningless and obfuscating, to reveal whatever significant might remain.

America saw a similar, parallel development of empiricism, though the focus of its practice was perhaps less sharp that in Britain. William James (1842-1910) formulated his radical pragmatism, a development of Charles Pierce's pragmatism, and presented it in *Pragmatism: A New Name for Some Old Ways of Thinking* in 1907. John Dewey (1859-1952) taught philosophy at the University of Chicago and Columbia University, and focused on issues of education and ethics. He proposed and developed an instrumentalist/pragmatic, or what he called a naturalistic empiricist, interpretation of and approach to these topics.

Philosophy is nothing if not argument, and the empiricists argued, at least initially, against the idealists of the time. The idealists are perhaps less well known, and fewer are known, than the empiricists. Their work constituted the last dwindling foil to the ascendant and increasingly sophisticated empiricism. We must look further back, and further abroad, to find these philosophers against which empiricism rebelled. Samuel Taylor Coleridge (1772-1834), the English poet and critic, was also a formidable philosopher. He almost single-handedly brought the philosophical romanticism of German Kantianism to England. He studied in Germany briefly, and read Kant's work. The American Ralph Waldo Emerson (1803-1882) "found inspiration in Coleridge,"[ix] and in 1836 published *Nature,* which expounded his idealist philosophy. Back in England, F. H. Bradley (1846-1924) published *Appearance and Reality* (1893) and *Essays on Truth and Reality* (1914), in which he worked out his absolute idealism. And in Germany, Ernst Cassirer (1874-1945), though not an idealist *per se,* was, as a neo-Kantian, much more sympathetic to the idealists. These philosophers represented the dwindling stream of transcendent, idealist, metaphysical philosophy at the turn of the century, at about the time Barfield was born in 1898, grew up, studied, went to school, and started on philosophical and literary careers spanning seventy-seven years. It is to the former career that we now turn.

II

The trend of academic philosophy in the 1920's was clearly and strongly toward radical empiricism. This impulse was for the most part a continuation of the work of David Hume. In 1739 Hume published *A Treatise of Human Nature,* the subtitle of which was *Being an Attempt to Introduce the Experimental Method of Reasoning into Moral Subjects.* Hume stated that the whole of his three volume treatise, over six hundred pages, was devoted to "the *full* examination of this question" regarding the fact that "all simple ideas and impressions resemble each other."[x] He expressed this fact in the proposition,

> That all our simple ideas in their first appearance are deriv'd from simple impressions, which are correspondent to them, and which they exactly represent.[xi]

In *An Abstract,* published in 1740 as a simplified presentation of the chief argument of his *Treatise,* he stated the implication of the proposition above:

> We can never think of any thing which we have not seen without [i.e., outside or external to] us, or felt in our own minds.[xii]

He added,

> This proposition seems to be equivalent to that which Mr. [John] Locke has taken such pains to establish, viz. that no ideas are innate.[xiii]

Except for mathematical knowledge, all other knowledge, for Hume, was the "assurance arising from the comparison of ideas,"[xiv] which in turn are derived from sense impressions, which are dependent on the faculties of sense, which are fallible. Therefore, said Hume, no knowledge of the world is indubitable.

For whatever reasons, philosophers in the late nineteenth and early twentieth centuries sought to establish *and give priority to* the status of empirical philosophy that Hume had formulated. Idealism is a system wherein truth claims, and matters of fact, are adjudicated on the basis of ideals, or abstract, intangible, transcendent principles. But such principles are not easily accessed, nor are the characterizations of them consistent from one idealist philosopher to another. Some philosophers, fed up with the unresolvable debates of metaphysics, traced this state of affairs to that inaccessibility of principles. If the objects of one's claims can be pointed to, there would be no argument.

Empiricists, including Russell, Moore, James, and others, had to fight their way free of the perspectives of idealism. Different philosophers began their empiricism with experience, but applied that criterion to different elements of the prevailing thought. Wittgenstein, for instance, focused on the nature of logical propositions in his *Tractatus*. He argued that logical propositions were tautologous or analytic. They were constructs of definition that needed no reference to the world for their truth content. As such, logical propositions had no significance insofar as one sought knowledge of the world. For that sort of knowledge, as Hume had argued almost two hundred years previous, one depended on the five senses.

In the early 1920's in Vienna, logical positivism as such was born. It began as a group of intellectuals—scientists, mathematicians, physicists, and others—with a strong group identity and mission.[xv] This group was self-consciously dedicated to developing and establishing an approach to the world they variously called "Logical Empiricism," "Scientific Empiricism," and "Logical Positivism."[xvi] In the preceding decade, including the time of World War I, Bertrand Russell, G.E. Moore, Ludwig

Wittgenstein, and others were discussing the role of logical analysis in science, philosophy, and human communications. In particular, Russell and Moore

> not only agreed on rejecting idealism, they also agreed on the reasons for doing so: first, because of its constructivism—because it holds minds to construct their experience rather than to contemplate it; second, because of its monism…. they both held that the universe is a collection of wholly independent, discrete entities and that "analysis" is the method by which we can come to know the nature of these atomic entities.[xvii]

The fruit of their work constituted the further radical development of empiricism. Not only was observation, or sense experience, the only basis for knowledge of the physical world, but knowledge of any other sort was not knowledge at all, save for mathematics. If a proposition could not be traced back to immediate sense experience, then either it was a logical proposition and thus a tautology, or it was sheer nonsense. Metaphysical, religious, and aesthetic judgments, such as "God is love," "the beautiful is transcendent," and so forth were not only not significant, but downright meaningless.

As the "revolt against idealism" became more apparently a rout, empirical philosophers turned their attentions more and more to the details of observation, empirical verification, and the language used to communicate such observations and verification. From this impulse grew linguistic analysis on the one hand and perceptual psychology on the other.

In 1928, while all of the above was still being worked out and worked on, Faber and Gwyer, Ltd. published a book dealing with…meaning. It was entitled *Poetic Diction: A Study in Meaning*[xvii] by Owen Barfield. Barfield was 30. He had earned a B.Litt. from Oxford, the thesis for which made up the basis for *Poetic Diction.* In this study of meaning, Barfield argued that words change meaning over time; that the effect of true poetic diction turns on the production of a "felt change of consciousness" on the reader's part; that this felt change of consciousness is fundamentally a change from the normal consciousness of the reader to that of the author of the poetic text; and that the change in consciousness in turn is effected by the meaning of the words and phrases of the poetic text, words and phrases that different meanings from today.

> To allow oneself, for instance, to experience to the full the wealth of meaning that the little epithet *trim* contained for Milton, is to see the world through his eyes in a specially intimate way.[xix]

As a result of his study of the history of language and changes in meaning, Barfield distinguished two fundamental sorts of meaning: given meaning, and created meaning. A poet, for example, or scientist, theologian or politician creates meaning when he constructs a new metaphor, and the connection that the metaphor makes is eventually considered as part of the word's meaning. The English language bristles with such words and meanings.[xx]

Given meaning will not be elucidated as easily. An instance, the instance, of given meaning is the myths of the world. Myths

> were not the arbitrary creations of 'poets', but the natural expression of man's being and consciousness at the time. The primary 'meanings' were *given,* as it were, by Nature.... Not man was creating, but the gods—or, in psychological jargon, his 'unconscious'.[xxi]

Meaning was not deduced or determined by convention, but was perceived. On the other hand, poetic diction *qua* poetic is the exercise of creating meaning—taking the given meaning of words, and extending and transferring that meaning. Insofar as metaphor performs this function, then there was no such thing as "metaphor" at this stage of the development of any particular language.

What were the implications for empiricism and logical positivism of Barfield's claims? Did the given/created distinction, or the fact that meanings change over time, have any significant relation to the doctrines of logical positivism, and the distinction between the language of logic and mathematics, on the one hand, and propositions verifiable by empirical observation on the other? Barfield thought that it did.

Barfield argued that two assumptions were critical to the doctrines of logical positivism: One was that meaning as expressed in language, in words, began as discrete elements, specifically the names of material objects. The other assumption was the unchanging nature of the world: it began as a solid material, is a solid material today, and will remain a solid material in the future. Barfield thought these assumptions were germane insofar as logic focuses on the *form* of words rather than primarily the meaning, and that philosophy was still considered

> a kind of offspring of Logic. To anyone attempting to construct a metaphysic in strict accordance with the canons and categories of formal Logic, the fact that the meanings of words change, not only from age to age, but from context to context, is certainly interesting; but it is interesting *solely* because it is a nuisance.[xxii]

Based on these assumptions, the logical positivist had no problem, by virtue of privileging empirical observation as *the* way to distinguish between meaningful statements and tautologies or mere definitions, determining that metaphoric language was of the latter sort. Much in Plato's dialogues, and practically the whole of St. Augustine's work, fell under the rubric of metaphor, and could justifiably be ignored.

But this produced a problem for the positivist, to the degree that they countenanced history in their philosophy: based on the criterion of verifiability, then the texts that pass that test are fewer and fewer the older they are, to the point that almost none of the earliest texts would pass, being entirely figurative. How can this be, that language *started* as wholly figurative? They could not have been saying *anything* meaningful to one another for millennium!

The answer was that the records were incomplete. Before the deluge of myth, the "disease of language" as Max Muller called it, a culture or race must have existed that spoke a literal and meaningful language. The words of this language referred to the same sorts of things that meaningful words today apply to: sensible, material objects, and *only* sensible, material objects. Some time after this, then, a culture of poetry rose up, in which this literal, empirically verifiable language was metaphorically applied wholesale. The word "breath" was applied to a feeling of the numinous, and meant "spirit." The word "crooked" was used to describe the merchant who cheated. The word "understand" was fashioned to call to mind how the disciple stood at the foot of the teacher's dais. These are the first of the oldest extant texts today.

Barfield regarded the supposition of a master race of poets arbitrary and absurd. There was no evidence for it, he claimed, and it was contrary to the direction of development of language throughout history, which was from almost wholly figurative in the oldest texts, to progressively more literal in the more recent texts. Barfield concluded that on the basis of the study of the history of language, given the positivist assumption regarding meaning and empirical verification,

> you may imply, if you choose…that the earliest words in use were 'the names of sensible, material objects' *and nothing more*—only, in that case, you must suppose the 'sensible objects' themselves to have been something more; you must suppose that they were not, as they appear to

be at present, isolated, or detached, from thinking and feeling.[xxiii]

Judging from textual evidence, and on the phenomenon of the felt change of consciousness that marks poetic diction *as* poetic, the making of meaning is, through time, more and more in the control of the individual human being.

III

Barfield forcefully engaged logical positivism in its linguistic aspects, but there was also the more distinctly psychological concern of the developing empiricism, and that had to do with the nature of perception itself. This concern grew from the preoccupation with formulating a workable version of perhaps the founding proposition of positivism: the empiricist criterion of meaning. Carl G. Hempel states

> The fundamental tenet of modern empiricism is the view that all non-analytic knowledge is based on experience. Let us call this thesis the principle of empiricism.[xxiv]

If a statement is not analytic, if it isn't a sort of definition or axiom of mathematics or geometry, then if it is to be regarded as knowledge, it must be founded on experience. Hempel continues, though:

> Contemporary logical empiricism has added to it the maxim that a sentence makes a cognitively meaningful assertion, and thus can be said to be either true of false,

only if it is either (1) analytic or self-contradictory or (2) capable, at least in principle, of experiential test.[xxv]

From this comes the conclusion that most of metaphysics and epistemology—the study of what constitutes knowledge, and how humans acquire that knowledge—are "devoid of cognitive significance—however rich some of them may be in non-cognitive import by virtue of their emotive appeal or the moral inspiration they offer."[xxvi] The testability criterion, though, was vague enough to attract the attention of positivists and non-positivists alike, and the positivists worked out various detailed developments.

One of those developments was actually a quite profound one, which Barfield took advantage of in *Saving the Appearances* in developing his own evolution of consciousness. The empirical criterion of meaning was qualified so that, rather than having to be traced back to an actual observation, a statement was meaningful if it could be traced to an observation that was not actual but was, in principle, possible. For instance, the statement, "A piece of paper is flammable," can be verified by direct observation: take a piece of paper, light a match to it, and observe the results. On the other hand, the truth-value of the statement, "there are mountains on the farther side of the moon,"[xxvii] could, for A. J. Ayer in 1936 who used it an example, be verified by direct observation. "But I do know what observations would decide it for me, if, as is theoretically conceivable, I were once in a position to make them."[xxviii] And with this statement at least, someone was in a position to make those direct observations. Even for A. J. Ayer in 1936, that statement was significant (not because it turned out to be true, by the way, but because even in 1936 there was a conceivable way of determining whether or not it was true).

Idealism fared much worse under the positivist scrutiny than did the possibility of space travel.

On the other hand, such a metaphysical pseudo-proposition as "the Absolute enters into, but is itself incapable of, evolution and progress," is not even in principle verifiable. For one cannot conceive of an observation which would enable one to determine whether the Absolute did, or did not, enter into evolution and progress.[xxix]

Ayer's example was "a remark taken at random from *Appearance and Reality*, by F. H. Bradley,"[xxx] whom we mentioned above. Years later, though, key phrases of the various formulations of the principle of empiricism, like "in principle" and "observable" had to be made more detailed and specific. "Observable" became "directly observable." Then the focus turned toward the objects of observation themselves. How do we know that what we see is not an illusion, or distorted somehow? In fact, empiricists employed the empiricist criterion of meaning for this very purpose.

Nonetheless, some began setting for themselves riddle such as these:

Let us consider Johannes Kepler: imagine him sitting on a hill watching the dawn. With him is Tycho Brahe. Kepler regarded the sun as fixed: it was the earth that moved. But Tycho followed Ptolemy and Aristotle in this much at least: the earth was fixed and all other celestial bodies moved around it. Do Kepler and Tycho see the same thing in the east at dawn?[xxxi]

Such a question was "the beginning of an examination of the concepts of seeing and observation."[xxxii] Such an examination referred in many cases to various optical illusions and visual puzzles being studied by psychologists. These included drawings of cubes, animals, and other figures, wherein two very different objects could be distinguished, but only one at a time. So one person may see a box figure as if from below, and another as if from above. One person may see an old lady in this figure, and another sees a young woman. One sees rabbits, another antelope.

More sophisticated, and telling, examples were of the type given above, regarding Kepler and Brahe, and given by Thomas Kuhn in *The Structure of Scientific Revolutions.* For instance, two different people look at the same piece of scientific equipment. One sees a glass gismo, another sees an X-ray tube with cathode and anode and a vacuum in between. Then there are examples of "mistakes" of observation, wherein the observer "sees" one thing, and then on closer or additional observation, "realizes" that it is something else. Or an example wherein an observer "hears a sound," but only after a few seconds can even put a name to it.

One interesting and profound conclusion reached by both philosophers and scientists in such examinations was that to some degree perception involves thinking—perception involves conception. For the empiricist, this is a rather upsetting turn of events. Insofar as thinking and perceiving are regarded as not only distinct but also separate, then observations can be the basis of the verifiability of a statement that purports to say something of the world. If it is to be a significant statement, if it is to be meaningful at all, its claim, whatever that may be, cannot be determined by logic, by thinking, but must be verifiable by perception. But what does one do if it turns out that observation itself has an inextricable conceptual element? Observation cannot be the independent arbiter of truth claims that the positivists thought it was.

The following chapters look more fully at Owen Barfield's philosophy, as he articulated it in *Saving the Appearances.* I hope it will be clear in these chapters that Barfield's philosophy therein does not end with the conclusions of perceptual psychology, but in fact only *begins* there, and from there sets out on a wild, interesting, credible and compelling journey.

Saving the Appearances:
A Study in Idolatry

In *Saving the Appearances: A Study in Idolatry*[xxxiii] Owen Barfield argued that Western reality consists of objects, and nothing else. These objects are idols because they are no longer representational; they no longer have an inside, a meaning which they mediate. The things style themselves as independent of human consciousness. Representations that no longer are acknowledged as such are rightly called idols, "hollow pretenses of life."

> They [have] no 'within.' 'They have mouths, and speak not: eyes have they, and see not. They have ears, and hear not: noses have they, and smell not. They have hands, and handle not: feet have they, and walk not: neither speak they through their throat.'[xxxiv]

His objective in *Saving the Appearances* was "to demonstrate on general grounds the necessity of smashing the idols,"[xxxv] and to save the appearances, the representations, as representational. His task was to first demonstrate that the appearances of the everyday, familiar world were in fact representational, though they were not recognized as such. To smash the idols would free the phenomena—the appearances of the everyday familiar world—to be expressive, and thereby restore to us a relationship with a psychic and voluntary other that is represented in the phenomena.[xxxvi]

The start of his project of demolition, he directed the reader to the foundation of the house of Western materialist reality, namely,

> what physical science has for a long time stressed, the enormous difference between what [physical science] investigates as the actual structure of the universe, including the earth, and the phenomena, or appearances, which are presented by that structure to normal human consciousness.[xxxvii]

If one accepts that premise that there is an enormous difference between the appearances or representations on the one hand, and what is really there,—what Barfield called "the unrepresented"[xxxviii]—on the other, then one must accept that the familiar world, "the world which is apprehended, not through instruments and inference, but simply," is "a system of collective representations."[xxxix]

> The time comes when one must either accept this as the truth about the world or reject the theories of physics as an elaborate delusion. One cannot have it both ways.[xl]

If one accepts that the fundamental level of reality is imperceptible to human senses, then what is in fact perceptible must be of a different nature than that fundamental base. The task of *Saving the Appearances* was to show the consequences of such a premise. Barfield sketched out what he took to be the implications of that premise.

If one is not seeing the world as it really is, as our common (scientific) sense tells us, then somehow the observer and what really is interact to produce or give rise to the familiar world of appearances. First, the reality, which is independent of us and our representations of it, "the unrepresented," must somehow give rise to sensations in us.

> In the conversion of raindrops into a rainbow, or (if you prefer it) the production of the rainbow out of them, the eye plays a no less indispensable part than the sunlight— or than the drops themselves. In the same way, for the conversion of the unrepresented into a representation, at least one sentient organism is a sine qua non as the unrepresented itself; and for the conversion of the unrepresented into representations even remotely resembling our everyday world, at least one nervous system organized about a spinal cord culminating in a brain, is equally indispensable.[xli]

Since "I can no[t]…merely smell 'coffee' [nor] hear 'a thrush singing,'[xlii] then sensations are somehow figured into recognizable objects. Assuming, as physical science does, an unrepresented, one does not, and cannot, smell coffee with senses only. To smell coffee involves more than mere sensation, and more than the "unrepresented."[xliii]11 This activity, in addition to sensation, Barfield called "figuration."[xliv]

> It is all that in the representations which is not sensation. For, as the organs of sense are required to convert the unrepresented into sensations for us, so something is required in us to convert sensations into 'things.'[xlv]

Barfield distinguished two other activities necessary for the coming together of the familiar world: "alpha-" and "beta-thinking."[xlvi] Alpha-thinking is to think about the representations, "and to speculate about or investigate their relations with each other."[xlvii] For example, one hypothesizes how pollution effects the ozone layer of the earth's atmosphere.

One focuses on the appearances as objects independent of the observer and one another. Beta-thinking is to "think about the nature of collective representations as such, and therefore their relation to our own minds."[xlviii] For instance, one may consider differences in primatological studies done by men, and those done by women. Such a study explicitly focuses on the role of human cognition and conceptualization on the nature of the observations.

The acceptance of an unrepresented implicates our minds in the production of the familiar world as collective representations, collective as language and habit and social structure, among other ways and means. The observer "participates in the phenomena."[xlix] This participation—figuration—is for the most part unconscious: when thinking about the representations—when alpha-thinking—

> our very attitude is, to treat [the representations] as independent of ourselves; to accept their 'outness' as self-evidently given.[l]

Figuration is distinct from alpha-thinking, but because figuration is for the most part unconscious, the line between figuration and alpha-thinking cannot be drawn precisely—if figuration is acknowledged at all. For instance: one sees something far off and thinks it is one thing, but upon a closer look sees that it is really something else. Was the observer mistaken in their alpha-thinking, in their thinking about, one representation, or did figuration present two representations?[li] This kind of event points up the similarity and close relationship between alpha-thinking and figuration. In other, this points up the close relationship between thinking about the nature of things, and how those things appear to one. Is it thinking, or is it perception?

Barfield stated that this question was implicit in the work of anthropologists studying the thought of so-called primitive peoples, [lii] and suggested the issues of participation and figuration as social and historical questions. The question was there phrased, "Can there be such a thing as '*They* thought *they* saw?'"[liii] If commonality is "the generally accepted criterion of the difference between 'I thought I saw' and 'I found it was,'" then how does one distinguish figuration from alpha-thinking, or, "representations [from] beliefs about representations"?[liv]

> How, then, if the 'they' are a whole tribe or population? If the 'mistake' is not a momentary but a permanent one? If it is passed down for centuries from generation to generation? If, in fact, it is never followed by a 'they found it was'? The difficulty is, that then the 'mistake' is itself a collective representation.[lv]

"Primitives" seem to evidence different figuration; but historically speaking, the ancient Greeks, for instance, and medievals, surely evidence different figuration, judging by the evidence of their view of the world that is available: texts, illuminations, paintings. There was not, for a long, long time, a "they found it was." There were gods, goddesses, angels, humours, the influences of stars and planets on the growth and character of plants, animals and humans. This is a "history of phenomena—that is, the history of the familiar world."[lvi] There is no recourse to the world of the ancients apart from their texts, which portrays that world, their "familiar world."[lvii]

*Original Participation*Barfield described participation as "an extra-sensory relation between man [sic] and the phenomena."[lviii] He referred to the anthropology of the day to illustrate this participation. Lucien Levy-Bruhl's *How Natives Think* illustrated Barfield's suggestion that with different collective representations "we are in contact with a different kind of thinking and a different kind of perceiving altogether."[lix]27 Levy-Bruhl described primitive thinking as

> essentially synthetic. By this I mean that the syntheses that compose it do not imply previous analyses of which the result has been registered in definite concepts…In

other words, the connecting links of the representations are given, as a rule, in the representations themselves.[lx]

There is nothing behind to a particular mythical tribal story, nothing that explains isolated parts of the story parallel but independent of the story itself. The explanations are the story itself: clouds are not thought to be the breath of the gods, but are rather perceived as such. This reading follows if the reports from primitive peoples (or the texts of ancient peoples) are our only evidence of their worldview. Barfield claimed that no shred of evidence existed that the informants (or authors) were attempting to explain anything, but were rather recording what they perceived. Whereas moderns do attempt to explain, in terms of elementary particles, their familiar world, and since those particles are practically and theoretically imperceptible, then moderns are detached from the bedrock of the real, and the primitives are (or ancients were) not.

Levy-Bruhl concluded that primitives "see with eyes like ours, but they do not perceive with the same minds."

> It is at a later stage [than the primitive] of social evolution that what we call a natural phenomenon tends to become the sole content of perception to the exclusion of the other elements...[lxi]

Barfield elaborated:

> in the act of perception, [primitives] are not detached, as we are, from the representations. For us the only connection of which we are conscious is the external one through the senses. Not so for them...It is not only a different alpha-thinking but a different figuration, with which we have to do, and therefore the phenomena are treated as collective representations produced by that different figuration.[lxii]

For Barfield, the most important difference between contemporary Western figuration and that of the primitives was "an awareness which we no longer have, of an extra-sensory link between the percipient and the representations."[lxiii] This kind of participation which obtained for ancients Barfield termed "original," the essence of which was that

> there stands behind the phenomena, and on the other side of them from me, a represented which is of the same nature as me...not mechanical or accidental, but psychic and voluntary.[lxiv]

Barfield was careful to suggest that this relationship did not imply dualism, two realities parallel to one another, with some inscrutable connection between the two. This is classically illustrated in Rene Descartes' distinction between mind a body. The body, he said, has extension in space, and can be measured and perceived. The mind does not have extension, and cannot be perceived. The history of philosophy and thought in general is in a sense a progressive unpacking of the implications of this distinction: since they are truly distinct, are they truly separate? If so, how are they related, and what influences do they exert on one another? If the mind is not material, how can it influence the body? If it cannot, then why even bother considering it in the investigation of the material world?

Barfield's psychic, voluntary other was not the same as Descartes "mind," and this fact is the hallmark of original participation: that psychic voluntary other *is perceived*, not deduced. The problem is that for the modern consciousness such an other is usually deduced, not perceived. Barfield stated clearly that the consciousness of the ancient was predominantly perceptual rather than conceptual; meaning was perceived, and not deduced. That the represented can be behind the representation is no more problematic than the fact that the window is behind the curtain. If the curtain is lace, then one can see both the curtain and the window behind the curtain at the same time.

Figuration is "the percipient's own contribution to the representation. It is all that in the representation which is not sensation."[lxv] Insofar as the represented appeared as external, then for the participant "there is no question of conscious figuration."[lxvi] Figuration for original participation was conscious; further, it involved "an awareness of...an extra-sensory link between the percipient and the representations."[lxvii] That activity, that figuration, was itself perceived as outside the percipient.

How could the wandering Hebrews sculpt a golden calf with their own hands, and then worship the calf as if it were an independent god? They perceived that figuration, but did not control it. One finds this hard to understand. But clearly this was the case, evident in the statements and exhortations exemplified by Isaiah 2:8, Habbabuk 2:18-19, Hosea 8:6, and especially Isaiah 44:9-20, which all direct the Israelite's attention to their own hands, as if they required to be exhorted to attend. Today one might do the same, but with the mind rather than the hands.

The explanation of what is an extra-sensory link goes something like this: The ancients were more focused on, attentive to, aware of, emotional and intuitive aspects of their surroundings, like one 'being aware' that someone is watching one, or standing behind one. Only, one has to work hard to avoid explaining away this awareness by reducing it to 'I felt a slight breeze on the back of my neck' or 'I sensed a slight increase in [air pressure/temperature/etc.].' Such explanations may or may not be true, that the air was disturbed, or that one's skin/hearing is sensitive to such minute changes. Even granted a sensation, the representation 'there is someone watching me'—apart from turning around to look, to receive more sensations—is still itself not sensation. The following exemplify the ancient response:

> Yoga is the control of thought waves in the mind-stuffAnd grief came upon Peleus' son, and his heart within his shaggy breast was divided in counsel, whether to draw his keen blade from his thigh and set the company aside

and so slay Atreides, or to assuage his anger and curb his soul.

And suddenly he felt the Eye. There was an eye in the Dark Tower that did not sleep. He knew that it had become aware of his gaze. A fierce eager will was there. It leaped towards him; almost like a finger he felt it, searching for him. Very soon it would nail him down, know just exactly where he was.

The first passage is from the Yoga Sutras of Patanjali, Chapter I.1. The second is from Homer's *Iliad*, Book I. The third is from Tolkien's *The Fellowship of the Ring*.[lxviii] These texts are not simply very figurative in their language, but *that is all that they are*. Abstractions and generalities are not evident at all. Though anyone today could write such passages, and in fact Tolkien has, in the authentically originally participatory texts one never finds the explanation, the real or literal sense of the figurative language in addition to and independent of the original text.[lxix]

One encounters a present expression of this sort of figurative vocabulary when speaking with a very devout, religious person, someone for whom what sounds to other ears as metaphor and figure of speech is the speech of everyday. Mother Theresa once said in an interview[lxx] that she was simply "a little pencil in his hand," that "poverty for us is a freedom," and "I find the rich much poorer." The interviewer asked,

"What are your plans for the future?"

"Tomorrow has not come. We have only today to love Jesus."

"And the future of the order?"

"It is his concern."

There comes a point with many such people beyond which the figures of speech and the metaphors are not reduced, by the speaker, to a literal and thereby real and true translation. Apparently Barfield encountered the ancient texts in a similar way.

Barfield considered primitive thought for the sake of illustration more than for argument.[lxxi] He regarded historically early humanity, as exemplified in texts such as the above, as a certain case of participation.[lxxii] Etymology directly presents original participation.

> All the evidence from etymology and elsewhere goes to show that the further back we penetrate into the past of human consciousness, the more mythical in their nature do the representations become.[lxxiii]

In *Poetic Diction* he said:

> Now it is an indisputable fact that, the further we look back into the history of the meanings of common words, the more closely we find them approximating to [a]...concrete type.[lxxiv]

Barfield argued that the concrete type of meaning made more sense of textual evidence than did Max Müller's "monosyllables with general meanings ('roots')."[lxxv] Barfield considered Müller's work the source of the received view that language developed in a way analogous to building a house from bricks. He claimed that etymology did not reveal Müller's roots, nor even suggest such things. Instead, what one finds is speech that is more and more figurative—less abstract—the older is the text.

> We can hear in the Greek *pneuma* an echo of just such an old, concrete, undivided meaning. This meaning...is lost in the inevitably double English rendering of spirit...and wind

> We must, therefore, imagine a time when...*pneuma*, or older words from which [this] had descended, meant neither breath, nor wind, nor spirit, nor yet all three of these things, but when [it] simply had [its] own peculiar meaning, which has since, in the course of the evolution of consciousness, crystallized into the three meanings specified—and no doubt into others also...[lxxvi]

Barfield regarded Müller's hypothesis of roots of speech as arbitrary and absurd. It was arbitrary because the general and obvious trend was from abstract and general meanings to increasingly figurative, concrete meanings. There was no warrant to hypothesize a time before the earliest texts—prehistory—in which that trend was completely reversed. The hypothesis was absurd because Müller argued, from the figurative—i.e., metaphorical—nature of the earliest meanings that the roots that preceded them were names of sensible objects only, and were later applied to insensible or spiritual qualities. If so, where did the insensible or spiritual qualities come from?

Why do the earliest meanings look merely material/figurative, e.g., gods and goddesses, rather than abstract, e.g., forces of nature? Barfield wrote:

> these poetic, and apparently 'metaphorical' values were latent in meaning from the beginning. In other words, you may imply, if you choose,…that the earliest words in use were 'the names of sensible, material objects' and nothing more—only, in that case, you must suppose the 'sensible objects' themselves to have been something more; you must suppose that they were not, as they appear to be at present, isolated, or detached, from thinking and feeling.[lxxvii]

These are concrete, individualized meanings, apparently blending what is today called material and immaterial, sensible and abstract, objective and subjective. Because of this apparent blending, the contemporary mind concludes that such language—e.g., of gods and goddesses—must have been deliberately metaphorical, because, after all, there are no such things as gods and goddesses.

It was not until the time of the Greeks, said Barfield, that the advent of alpha-thinking—of a thinking about the representations in and of themselves, a deliberate overlooking of the extra sensory connection—was evident, though the representations thought about at that time were participated phenomena, the only sort of representations available.[lxxviii]

> Apart from speculative thought, it would never have occurred to an ancient Greek to doubt that the heavenly

bodies and their spheres were in one way or another repre-sentations of divine beings.[lxxix]

And according to Barfield, that original participation "survived in an attenuated form even into the Middle Ages."[lxxx]

Idolatry

If representations are correlative to figuration and alpha-thinking, then participation must have been different in the past, since the repre-sentations were so different. Barfield argued that the mythical nature of representations of ancient humankind made this evident. The modern picture of this development was quite to the contrary.

> For the nineteenth-century fantasy of early man first gazing, with his mind *tabula rasa*, at natural phenomena like ours, then seeking to explain them with thoughts like ours, and then 'peopling' them with the 'aery phantoms' of mythology, there is just not any single shred of evidence whatever.[lxxxi]

The familiar world of the ancients was a different world from the con-temporary one.

Then alpha-thinking begins to change things, literally. In alpha-thinking "we must necessarily be aware of ourselves (that is, of the self which is doing the thinking) as sharply and clearly detached from the thing thought about".[lxxxii] If one considers critically what influences one's way of thinking about the world, one must assume some distance between the world and one's thinking about the world, and further, one must assume a distance between, on the one hand, the world and one's thinking about the world, and on the other hand, the one that is draw-ing that first distinction. Both these are movements of detachment, and only differ in the direction. The former movement—of detaching from the phenomena—is Barfield's alpha-thinking; the latter movement—of detaching from the phenomena and one's thinking about them—is Barfield's beta-thinking. In both cases there is assumed a discontinuity between the observer and the observed. With the systematic practice of alpha-thinking, first noticeable in ancient astronomy, original participation—that awareness of a connection between the phenomena and the percipient being—is eclipsed.

Though figuration and alpha-thinking as activities can be distinguished in theory—that is, by a little beta-thinking—representations and beliefs about representations cannot be sharply distinguished. How are they related? Alpha-thinking can influence figuration such that thoughts about the representations are "smitten into the representations themselves."[lxxxiii] This is so especially to the degree that one is unaware of figuration. This relation between figuration and alpha-thinking, over time, in history, is then a "history of consciousness, and of the collective representations which are its correlative."[lxxxiv] The death of original participation

> took place when Copernicus (probably—it cannot be regarded as certain) began to think, and others, like Kepler and Galileo, began to affirm that the heliocentric hypothesis not only saved the appearances, but was physically true. It was this, this novel idea that the Copernican (and therefore any other) hypothesis might not be a hypothesis at all but the ultimate truth, that was almost enough in itself to constitute the 'scientific revolution.'[lxxxv]

Given the relation between figuration and alpha-thinking, the present Western scientific collective representations were born

> when men began to take models, whether geometrical or mechanical, literally...The whole point of a machine is, that, for so long as it goes on moving, it 'goes by itself' without man's participation. To the extent therefore that the phenomena are experienced as a machine, they are believed to exist independently of man, not to be participated and therefore not to be in the nature of representations.[lxxxvi]

Alpha-thinking sunk into figuration, "enough to deprive the phenomena of those last representational overtones...which still informed them in the Middle Ages, and to eliminate from them the last traces of original participation."[lxxxvii] What are left are the "mechanomorphic collective representations which constitute the Western world to-day."[lxxxviii]

Those mechanomorphic collective representations are idols, said Barfield, and we are idolaters. "When the nature of artificial images are forgotten, they become idols."[lxxxix]

> By treating the phenomena of nature as objects wholly extrinsic to man…and then by endeavoring to deal with these objects as astronomy deals with the celestial appearances or physics with the particles, nineteenth-century science, and nineteenth-century speculation, succeeded in imprinting on the minds and imaginations of men their picture of an evolution of idols.[xc]

Denying that the familiar world—the appearances—were in some part of their own making, habitual practitioners of alpha-thinking committed idolatry. They rendered independent status to what was in some way dependent on their consciousness. The collective representations were taken to be machines, and their history was considered from this assumption; instead of an evolution of the familiar world, and a correlative evolution of consciousness, modern science wrote a history of idol matter in idol time through idol space. The end of this progression is idolatry, a worship of empty things, of nothing. Why did Barfield use a term so laden with religious meaning and history? The connection to the idolatry against which the Jews were commanded is that both kinds of idolatry lead to the emptying of the idolater. Insofar as percipients regard themselves as phenomenal, then they too are machines, empty of an interior that is qualitatively distinct from its exterior. A machine, further, is motivated from without, and runs on its own, rather than from within, (e.g., by the grace of God, or by the gods, or according to one's genius). In this way the habitual practitioner of alpha-thinking commits idolatry in the most grievous sense.

Barfield argued that the phenomena were representational for the Jews, and the tendency to seek therein that psychic and voluntary other—the tendency to original participation—was surely strong, and thus in need of the restraint and witness of the commandment. But they knew what the consequences were of worship of idols, idols that

> [have] no 'within.' 'They have mouths, and speak not: eyes have they, and see not. They have ears, and hear not: noses have they, and smell not. They have hands, and handle not: feet have they, and walk not: neither speak they through their throat.'[xci]

The consequence was that those who worshipped the idols became like them—with mouths but not speaking, eyes, but not seeing, etc..[xcii]

This refrain from original participation also began a movement of "concentration or centripetal deepening of participation,"[xciii] for though Jews were not to look for God in or through the phenomena, they were to look forward to a day when God would be found in a deeper place, in the I AM found in Jesus' "I am" sayings.

> As to the glories displayed in the 104th Psalm, God was no longer in them; they were no longer His representations or 'names.' For He had now only one name—I AM—and that was participated by every being who had eyes that saw and ears that heard and who spoke through his throat. But it was incommunicable, because its participation by the particular self which is at this moment uttering it was an inseparable part of its meaning. Everyone can call his idol 'God,' and many do; but no being who speaks through his throat can call a wholly other and outer Being 'I.'[xciv]

Thus in hearing Jesus'

> "I am—" sayings in St. John's Gospel: 'I am the way, the truth, and the life…."I am the light of the world…."I

and the Father are one...' and we shall reflect how near was the Aramaic dialect he spoke to Hebrew—...at each 'I am' the disciples must almost have heard the Divine Name itself, man's Creator, speaking through the throat of man; till they can hardly have known whether he spoke to them or in them, whether it was his voice which they heard or their own.[xcv]

Final Participation

Western idolatry, the result of habitual practice of alpha-thinking, threatens to leave the Westerner empty, just as the Jewish idolatry did those who worshipped false gods. But like them, the Westerner may yet participate the phenomena, this time from within themselves, as if co-creating the phenomena. Barfield thought that choices were few for avoiding emptiness, for "all the unity and coherence of nature depends on participation of one kind or the other."[xcvi] If the death of original participation was apparently inevitable at the hand of alpha-thinking latent in it, if one is to avoid total meaninglessness, then the West must again participate the phenomena.

But this participation has changed directions, as prophesied so to speak in Old Testament history: rather than the represented being on the other side of the phenomena from us, the represented is to be experienced "within ourselves,"[xcvii] as the source of the I AM. We are, said Barfield, whether we "like it or not, in...a 'directionally creator' relation" to the phenomena—to nature, the familiar world.[xcviii] The human-centered participation sketched out in the beginning of this chapter, in terms of an unrepresented, sensation, figuration, alpha-thinking, and beta-thinking, Barfield called "final participation."[xcix] The represented in this scheme is none other than humanity itself. Nature can no longer be representative of something on the other side of it from the percipient, but is representative of the person themselves. In this directionally-creator relation to the familiar world, "what so stands is not my poor temporal personality, but the Divine Name [the I AM] in the unfathomable depths behind it."[c] This is no call to a "riot of private and personal symbolisms"; it is a call to "strive humbly to create more nearly as [the Divine Name] creates."[ci] "The future of the phenomenal world can no longer be regarded as entirely independent of [human] volition."[cii]

The development from original participation to idolatry to final participation Barfield termed "the evolution of consciousness."[ciii] In Western human development this may be simply characterized as a move from an originally wholly perceptual unity of experience and awareness to the advent of thinking that focuses more and more on what one might call the sensory aspects of that original unity, such that the thinker is finally and wholly cut off from those aspects, to the present experience of an impulse to again participate the appearances. To further flesh out the skeleton of the evolution of consciousness as presented earlier, Barfield's work in etymology needs to be discussed more fully, for it is in the history of language that Barfield saw the most convincing evidence for an evolution of consciousness. The value of etymology was not in

> disputing about the proper meaning to be attached to a particular word in a sentence…But if we would consider the nature of meaning, and the relation between thoughts and things, we cannot profitably dispense with etymology.[civ]

By etymology one sees clearly, not specific meanings of words upon which one will base entire theories, but that meanings have changed. This is a study of the evolution of consciousness, and because language and consciousness are so intimately related, Barfield argued that from changes in language one may see changes in consciousness. For logicians the fact of changing meaning is more a nuisance than an interesting phenomenon to be dealt with fruitfully, but a consideration of the meaning of meaning must have an historical perspective. In Barfield's *History in English Words* and *Poetic Diction: A Study in Meaning,*[cv] as well as several chapters in *Saving the Appearances,* he explicitly discussed the history of language and meaning as the unfolding of evolving consciousness, of which it was shown "that the evolution of nature is correlative to the evolution of consciousness..."[cvi] Specifically, the

> Western type of consciousness may be said to have begun...with the emergence of Greek thought from the Orient. For the Western outlook is based essentially on that turning of [human] attention to the phenomena, which in this book has been called alpha-thinking.[cvii]

From another point of view,

> the evolution of consciousness can best be understood as a more or less continuous progress from a vague but immediate awareness of the 'meaning' of phenomena towards an increasing preoccupation with the phenomena themselves. The earlier awareness involved experiencing the phenomena as representations; the latter preoccupation involves experiencing them, non-representationally, as objects in their own right, existing independently of human consciousness.[cviii]

Given that the familiar world is a system of collective representations, and assuming language to be a part of that system, for it is mostly through language that we become aware of representations that one shares a world with others, then a look at language and meaning through history will show "the familiar world and human history lying together, bathed in the light of the evolution of consciousness."[cix]

To Barfield it was obvious from the written records of medieval Europe, for instance, that the person of the Middle Ages lived in a different world from ours.

> But we have here not merely to notice the fact that [the medieval person] expressed [themselves] in so different a manner and in such different terms from those which are natural to us, but to ask the question why [they] did so.[cx]

The mythic character of the oldest written human records, the literal, prosaic character of the sixteenth and seventeenth century literature, the

Romantic movement in poetry and criticism in the eighteenth century, the medieval illuminator who never hesitated to represent angels in every-day medieval garb, all attest to the differences of awareness of the world from one age to another.

> [i]n the eighteenth and nineteenth centuries men who wanted to paint or sculpt an angel...felt obliged to supply him with a special, unearthly gown...[cxi]

Why would this be? Barfield suggested that medievals' clothes were representational, like most everything else in their world, whereas "our clothes are prosaic, because our minds are literal."[cxii]

The modern attitude toward such medieval representationalism is that they simply confused the literal and symbolical. Barfield claimed instead they

> combined the two states of mind which we today mean by those words. Indeed, we shall find throughout that the main difficulty that prevents us from breaking through the idols to the actuality of history, that is, to the evolution of consciousness, lies in the fact that we go on using the same words without realizing how their meanings have shifted.[cxiii]

The evolution of consciousness, from original participation to idolatry to final participation, he alternatively describes as a movement from a vague but immediate awareness of the meaning of appearances (given meaning), to a preoccupation with the phenomena (no meaning), to the re-enlivening of the phenomena with meaning (created meaning).[cxiv] Meaning has changed, and thus, given the role of language as mediator of collective representations, the familiar world has changed also. Mythic language expresses "given meaning,"[cxv] in that it is a compulsive unity of speech and perception and thought and nature; language is representational, as are the phenomena themselves—language and phenomena are not yet wholly, or even nearly, distinct. Nature and thought are immediate and simultaneous and coextensive. Idolatry is the process, and the idols the products, of the splintering of that unity—nature from thought, and thought from things, and things from speech. Those things then are idols, and the attempt to break and crush those idols and restore to them a representational character is iconoclasm. This was the work of the Romantics of the eighteenth and nineteenth centuries, as Barfield saw it: their work was to re-vision the phenomena as phenomenal. The psychic and voluntary other was not to be found on the other side of the appearances. In what sense, then, were the phenomena representational?

> If nature is indeed 'dis-godded,' and yet we again begin to experience her, as Wordsworth did—and as millions have done since his time—no longer as dead but as alive; if there is no 'represented' on the far side of the appearances, and yet we begin to experience them once more as appearances, as representations—the question arises, of what are they representations?[cxvi]

Barfield answered, "Man." Immediately he asked, "But what is Man?" If all of nature has been dis-godded, and if our own bodies are part of nature, and therefore dis-godded, and we think of our selves as identical with our bodies, then

> the great change which the evolution of consciousness has brought about and the great lessons which [people] had begun to learn have all been wrenched awry...And all because we have not learnt—though our very physics shouts it at us—that nature herself is the representation of Man.[cxvii]

The Romantic poets and Impressionist painters taught that the human being is in a directionally-creator relation to the phenomena, in that the phenomena are representations of that human nature. For Barfield, those poets and painters served as reminders "that the rejection of original participation may mean, not the destruction but the liberation of images."[cxviii]

[T]hey really painted in the light of the eye, as no other painters had done before them. They were striving to realize in consciousness the normally unconscious activity of 'figuration' itself. They did not imitate; they expressed 'themselves'—inasmuch as they painted nature as the Representation of Man.[cxvix]

The Objectivity of Consciousness

If Barfield's argument in *Saving the Appearances* could be outlined (and the proof will be in the pudding), it would look something like this:

1. If it is true, as modern (i.e., post classical) physics postulates, that there is a sub-or super-sensible base of reality, which cannot be experienced as such, only inferred; and
2. if this base is all that is independently real or objective; and
3. since what one experiences as the familiar world, the cool breeze through the window, the gravelly sound of a car rolling through the alley, the smell of toast, even the prepared microscope slide in the laboratory, since this is sensible through and through; and
4. since experience is not mere sensation;
5. /∴ the familiar world of experience is not independent of human awareness or consciousness; further,
6. since collectivity, the corroboration by others, is the sufficient mark of reality with regard to the familiar world; and
7. since another way of putting premise 4 is that the phenomena of the familiar world are representations;
8. /∴ the familiar world is a system of collective representations, and the sub-or supersensible base is unrepresented (Barfield used the term "the unrepresented"); further,

9. since collective representations are correlative to the consciousness that experiences them; and

10. since language and art are two fundamental vehicles for the maintenance of the collectivity of the representations; and

11. since the older a language and associated arts, the greater the difference between them and those of today;

12. /:. the consciousness that experienced such different representations is different from the consciousness of today; further,

13. since the collective representations evident in language and art are the world, the real world, for the consciousness that is correlative to them;

14. the world of the older cultures was a different world from that of today.

Consciousness has changed, Barfield argued, and therefore so has the world, in the only sense of the world that is available to 20th century western humanity. The evolution of the world is correlative to the evolution of consciousness. Barfield used the anthropologist's, the medieval scholar's, and the ancient philosopher's term of "participation" for this correlation. A world, any world, is, on the account that posits a sub-or super-sensible base as the only "thing" independent of human consciousness, thereby correlative to consciousness. There is no world, any world, apart from consciousness.

With *Saving the Appearances* outlined in this fashion, a couple of things become more than obvious. One is the fact that Barfield did construct an argument. He did have premises, from which he drew various conclusions. The implication of this is that that argument is, *qua* argument, open to evaluation of its various premises and conclusions. Some pertinent objections of various premises and conclusions are taken up here, in this chapter, and the outcome granted in the following chapters.

A second matter made more perspicuous by outlining the argument of *Saving the Appearances* is the varied implications drawn from that argument, implications that go beyond the argument itself. It is not only important, and fruitful and interesting, to look in detail at the argument that Barfield made, but also to trace out whatever implications might follow from that argument, to see where Barfield's work can go. The ability to trace out those implications more than a few steps, and a few years into the future, will be difficult going, as with all such matters. Philosophy, and argumentation, and consciousness, have historical aspects to them, which are almost always impossible to anticipate ahead of time. What is perhaps easier to do, and still very valuable and important to do, is to trace out the implications more laterally, into other fields of study and other contemporary issues. Such is the work of the two chapters after the present one.

Objections

The first objection to Barfield's argument as outlined above regards the notion of the unrepresented, that sub-or super-sensible base of reality. If the fact of such an unrepresented is not granted, then the conclusions do not follow. The familiar world would not be, in any fundamental sense, the representation of human consciousness. Drop this premise, as does, for instance, Richard Rorty, the literary critic and philosopher who worked to raise chance and contingency to their rightful place in the human conversation, then there is no longer any philosophically interesting sense to the notion of other worlds. A closer look at the specifics of his criticism follows in the next chapter.

Alternatively, one could restrict the notion of an unrepresented to the intellectual field in which it was born—modern physics—and justify ignoring it in any and all other sorts of intellectual study on the grounds that it is merely a technical term and hypothetical notion. One can ignore the notion when doing history, anthropology, literary criticism, and philosophy. In these, and other, disciplines, one can proceed on the assumption of classical physics, namely, that reality is out there, absolutely independent of human awareness of it.

A third alternative is to suggest the question, What if one considers the notion of an unrepresented valid, for physics and other disciplines, but only and always as a working hypothesis, never as the way things really are? All bets are off; all conclusions necessarily and obviously tentative. This is the conventional wisdom. But what if one took this seriously, explicitly reminded oneself of it in every textbook and lecture, and treated the conclusions as the tentative notions they would necessarily be?

Barfield thought there were good reasons to think that these three alternatives were so unpalatable as to be simply unacceptable. The second alternative of compartmentalizing intellectual pursuits, for instance, would mean stripping any and all other intellectual disciplines of their borrowed assumption of an unrepresented. Each would have to stand on its own—no wholesale and uncritical borrowing from physics. Barfield thought that given the more or less deep commitment that most other intellectual disciplines had made to the concepts of physics, including an unrepresented, that if they were to give it all back, there would be no history, no philosophy, no anthropology, or very little left, which would be unrecognizable.

If this is not obvious, then Barfield reminded the reader of, for instance, the geologist's dependence on the concept of radioactivity in order to measure the age of rocks. This radioactivity assumes the fact of an unrepresented that, though one cannot see it or even picture it, the phenomena that the geologist measures is somehow real, which was real before humans ever measured it, and in fact is explicitly assumed to have been behaving millions of years ago just as it is now. One can restrict the notion of an unrepresented to physics, but will not be able to restrict physics itself to the laboratory or chalkboard.

The last alternative, to consider all of the conclusions of physics to be tentative and never more than that, is not consistent with the use of technology that is based on the science of physics. Engineering feats such as nuclear power, hydroelectric power, and silicon-based microprocessing certainly have not come about on the power of tentative hypotheses. They may not be directly dependent on the notion of an unrepresented, yet how would one determine otherwise?

An answer to that question is an answer also to the first alternative—drop the notion of an unrepresented altogether, if it is going to commit one to Barfield's evolution of consciousness. How does one determine what concepts and practical results of physics, and the other disciplines, really do depend on the notion of an unrepresented? Whether they do or not, that notion is a cardinal feature of the sciences, and the sciences have proven to be astoundingly successful as a tool for the manipulation of that unrepresented, or at least the phenomena that it, together with human consciousness, give rise to. Science works, and that utility is an imposing, if not sufficient, argument for its truth.

Barfield concluded that, granted the prevalence of the concepts and methods of physics, which goes well beyond strictly intellectual studies but right into the meanings of ordinary words, then the most reasonable alternative is to maintain the notion of an unrepresented and its implications, but to do so consistently, in and out of physics, in history and philosophy, literary criticism, and geology. As one exercises consistent application of the notion, one will learn better and more clearly just to what degree one is justified in trusting it. It may end up proving it. But clearly, adopting here, ignoring it there, assuming it now, forgetting it later, will only supply inconclusive and confusing results.

To be committed to the notion of an unrepresented and its implications for the understanding of the nature of reality and the phenomena, is what saying that the west today has a scientific worldview means. To the degree that this is true, therefore, the west is also committed to the implications, including that the familiar world is a system of collective representations. This includes when one does science—those phenomena are as correlative to consciousness as the smell of the spring wind on the mountaintop that sweeps the schoolboy away in romantic reverie. There is no question then what the world, the familiar world, really is: it is a system of collective representations, and the collective representations are "everything that is obvious."[cxx]

Grant the assumption when doing philosophy, when reading the ancient texts of Plato, Aristotle, Heraclitus, Plotinus, Augustine, those of Hildegard of Bingen, Thomas of Aquinas, and Francis Bacon, of Immanuel Kant, David Hume, John Locke and G.W. Leibniz, of F.H. Bradley, John Dewey, Edmund Husserl and Richard Rorty. There is no question what the world was, and is, for all these: it was, and is, all that they were, and are, aware of, evident in the texts that they left behind. Correlative to those representations was and is consciousness. There are no phenomena without consciousness.

To say that collective representations—the appearances of the familiar world corroborated by one's neighbors—are correlative to consciousness, is different from saying what was said in the last sentence of the previous paragraph: there are no phenomena without consciousness. Many people, including scientists and philosophers, admit that the familiar world today is partly the result of the nature of human consciousness. This admission comes in various forms, from the conclusions of perceptual psychology regarding perceptual judgment and the observer's education, training, and mood, to the conclusions of Barfield.

On the other hand, to say that there are no phenomena without consciousness is a quite different matter. Many believe that though consciousness and phenomena are correlative today, nonetheless, for the vastly greater part of the life of the earth and the universe, there have been phenomena, nature has existed, without consciousness. A world is imagined as having existed long before consciousness arose. If a human had been around, that person would have a found an earth possibly unrecognizable in shape, form, and composition, but it would still have been sensible and material.

Given Barfield's argument, one has to admit that only the unrepresented exists, and existed, independent of consciousness. Only the unrepresented existed before consciousness arose. Given the nature of the unrepresented, then there is absolutely nothing one can say about any phenomena before consciousness, because *there were none.* This is not what the evolutionary biologist, the geologist, and the astronomer implies or explicitly states. It looks to be literally absurd to talk about phenomena without the correlative consciousness. Either there was consciousness then, geological ages ago, or there was not. If not, then there simply were not phenomena to be observed. One may respond that with all such descriptions one *does* assume such a consciousness: *if* someone were there to observe, they would see what the geologists suggest would be there. Barfield makes to responses. One is to turn the empiricist's fundamental rule against their own suggestion: something in the past is not even in principle verifiable by observation, since it is impossible, even in principle, to travel back in time. The second response is: *If* someone were there in the remote past, to observe this wholly material origin of the world, *which* person would it be? A geologist living today? How about a medieval monk? Aristotle? Confucius? To protest any nomination but the first would simply bring the discussion of the issues back to where one started, namely, trying to determine the nature of the phenomena and the role that human consciousness plays in the sustaining of those phenomena. Is one to speak of the appearances of Aristotle, or those of a scientist living today? Is one to take back to that remote time the worldview of St. Thomas Aquinas, or of B.F. Skinner?

Saving the Appearances is clearly a critique of science. But Barfield made a distinction between "the actual doctrines of modern science and the collective representations to which the growth of science has contributed."cxxi Though the doctrines of contemporary quantum physics, for instance, are less reductively materialistic than those of its classical cousin, nevertheless the collective representations are—the familiar world is—mostly and principally material and mechanical. Quantum physicists are working out details of experimental results that seem to establish the involvement of the observer, and the experimental setup itself, in the heretofore independent phenomena, yet most in the west are reductive materialists.

Either one is forgetting what was learned from modern physics about the relation of the mind to the phenomena of nature, or one has decided that it is not relevant. If Barfield's argument is valid, though, then in either case, since a sub-or super-sensible base of the material, sensible world is assumed, consequently the only phenomena one knows are collective representations. Since one assumes the sub-or super-sensible base to have always existed, at least as far as the history of the earth is concerned, then one has to assume the same for all and any history of the world. Even if one continues to deny this, one has to admit that, though there was surely an unrepresented before the entrance of humans on the scene, nothing can be said about it, since such a description necessarily implies human consciousness. Any description of the world does not exist apart from consciousness, only the unrepresented does. The unrepresented does not appear; whereas the world is phenomenal through and through.

If, therefore, the notion of an unrepresented is accepted, then it necessarily follows that nature and consciousness are coeval. There never has been a world apart from consciousness. The following can now be added to the argument laid out at the beginning of this chapter:

15. since the only phenomena are collective representations; and
16. since any description of the world, as distinct from the unrepresented, implies consciousness correlative to it;
17. /:. "Consciousness is as real, and as old, as the so-called outer world of nature."[cxxii]

The world is representational. The world is an image, or a system of images. Barfield thought that, granting the representational nature of the familiar world, when one denies that the phenomena are images, then those images, which are images nonetheless, are better called idols.

Idols, suggested Barfield, are images that are mistaken as self-sufficient, self-sustaining, self-referential. So long as this denial is maintained, then the phenomena of nature are idols. So long as the denial itself is deemed unquestionable and irrevocable, that is justifiably called idolatry.

> Modern science is inseparable from the voluntary decision out of which it arose three or four centuries ago; namely, the decision to exclude what were called 'occult qualities' from its purview. Modern scientific *method* remains based on that rule, and technology owes all its strength to a rigid observance of it.[cxxiii]

Occult qualities are "qualities or forces which, although regarded as causally effective in the natural world, are not even in theory observable by the senses."[cxxiv] These are not considered when scientists do science. Such science depends on what Barfield called "alpha-thinking," which is a thinking about, a focus on the phenomena as independent. As such, alpha-thinking is a simultaneous and necessary interruption of conscious participation. To the degree that these occult or non-phenomenal qualities, the extra-sensory aspects of experience in the world, are understood as nothing more than subjective states and not as part of the objective world, then science denies participation. To the degree that one experiences the world in this way, composed of wholly independent objects over and against subjective experience, then one experiences a world made possible by science. One has a scientific worldview.

Occult qualities can be referred to as extra-sensory, immaterial, or abstract. One way to describe a world of conscious participation is one where extra-sensory, immaterial, or abstract qualities are experienced as in the world. Barfield contended that before alpha-thinking became habitual, experience of the world was like this. This experience was impulsive and instinctual, and the percipient did not make any regular and strict distinctions between these qualities and those that are today called material and sensible. Barfield called this way of experiencing the world original participation, original referring to the fact that it was the nature of the first human consciousness.

Barfield thought it was important to learn how to see the world in this way again, except that now the participation would have to be more deliberate, and would have to involve one's will in a way that it did not in original participation. Barfield wanted to help the reader experience those occult qualities. He thought that the place where such awareness was most significantly missing was in the modern picture of human and biological evolution. Barfield argued that the prevailing notion of evolution was a hypothesis made to explain the phenomena of the time, which was the latter half of the nineteenth century.

> What were the phenomena of nature at the time when the new doctrine began to take effect, and particularly at the Darwinian moment in the middle of the nineteenth century? They were *objects*. They were unparticipated to a degree which has never been surpassed before of since....What then had alpha-thinking achieved at precisely this point in the history of the West? It had temporarily set up the appearances of the familiar world...as things wholly independent of man....[cxxv]

It was to such objects that biology and geology, history and philosophy, applied their theorizing, their alpha-thinking. Thus alpha-thinking—thinking that preoccupies itself with the sense content of the appearances—was applied to the products of centuries of previous alpha-thinking. Barfield argued that on the basis of a study of language, it was clear that when Plato and Aristotle and the Greeks exercised alpha-thinking, and Barfield considered them the first systematic practitioners of alpha-thinking, they applied that alpha-thinking to participated phenomena. Those phenomena were of a very different sort than the phenomena to which Darwin and the scientists and intellectuals of his day applied their alpha-thinking. It was to phenomena already rendered non-representational by centuries of such preoccupation.

As a result, biology and geology, history and philosophy, assumed that objects, not representations or images, are what evolved. Evolution was "conceived mechanomorphically as a series of impacts of idols on other idols."[cxxvi] Barfield identified the essence of this evolution to be the absence of human participation, of consciousness. According to this picture, the vast majority of the earth's pre-history predated consciousness. Anterior to all was material. This was the background to those intellectual disciplines interested in the past, Barfield argued.

> The biological picture of evolution was imprinted, no less deeply than on other men's, on the minds of those scholars—etymologists, mythologists, anthropologists—who made it their business to study the human past, and it was accepted by them, not as speculation or hypothesis, but as established fact. It was the given framework into which they had to fit any theory they chose to form. It was treated as part of the appearances they were setting out to save.[cxxvii]

It is fair to include in this list of scholars philosophers and historians of philosophy. They assume a mechanomorphic, mindless, evolution prior to the appearance of human—or at least self-conscious—beings on the scene. For philosophers no less than for geologists and biologists, evolution is

> Treated as part of the appearances they are setting out to save. Consequently, in their endeavours to explain the mind of early…man, they set him down, in fancy, in front of phenomena identical with their own, but with his mind

tabula rasa, and supposed the origin of human consciousness to lie in his first efforts to speculate about those phenomena. In this way was evolved the doctrine of 'animism', according to which the fancy of primitive man had 'peopled' nature with spirits. Now, in order that nature may be peopled with spirits, nature must first be devoid of spirit; but this caused scholars no difficulty, because they never supposed the possibility of any other kind of nature. The development of human consciousness was thus presented as a history of alpha-thinking beginning from zero and applied always to the same phenomena, at first in the form of erroneous beliefs about them and, as time went on, in the form of more and more correct and scientific beliefs. In short, the evolution of human consciousness was reduced to a bare history of ideas.[cxxviii]

Barfield thought that an evolution of consciousness was an alternative to the picture described above.

Barfield concluded that Earth's prehistory as a history of only material was an illusion. The distinction between the unrepresented and the appearances of the familiar world was now known. When Darwinian evolution was suggested and developed, there was yet no intuition of such a distinction. Nearly everyone at that time who thought about the history of the world was an idolater in Barfield's sense. They assumed that what they studied had always been that way.

If Barfield is correct, then idolaters looked back into a fantasy land. What they saw was pure illusion. They denied the phenomena any representational status or nature. They did something like this:

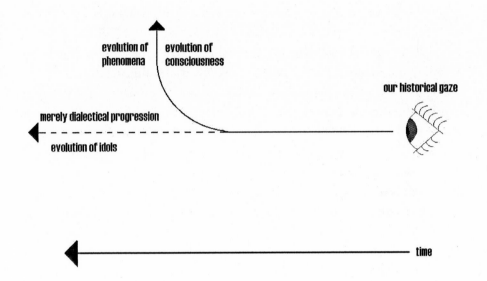

Barfield thought that such an imagined biological evolution drew the contemporary historical gaze away from the reality of the evolution of consciousness and phenomena. Once one let go of the false picture, Barfield argued, one could see that consciousness was as real and as old as the so-called outer world of nature. Consciousness is objective.

What difference does such a point of view make? After all, as Barfield himself pointed out, quantum physics, or at least the interpretations of quantum phenomena, was at a point of establishing the objectivity of consciousness. Perceptual psychology, too, had pretty well convinced many of the interconnection of thinking and perception, the involvement of human consciousness with the phenomena which is called the everyday world. Such notions did not, and have not disturbed historians of philosophy, nor philosophers in general. But neither quantum physics nor perceptual psychology is history or philosophy. Barfield is one of the few philosophers who has taken what is common to both quantum physics and perceptual psychology—that the objective world as one knows it, as there really is no way to think otherwise, is a world of consciousness—and then looked at human history and thinking in the light of that claim. Perceptual psychology has not done it, and neither has quantum physics. But philosophers should; and one has. At the very least, once this is done with care and with the various talents and insights in the community of philosophers, one can see whether or not it really is a workable notion for the study of human history. The following chapters look at the history of philosophy, and philosophers' view of history, in light of Barfield's argument above, drawing out yet more details of Barfield's own philosophy, as well as tracing out into traditional philosophy some implications of an evolution of consciousness.

Philosophy and Different Worlds

*I*It should be clear now that Barfield argued that consciousness and the familiar world were correlative, and changes in the one signaled or reflected changes in the other. Alpha-thinking, the thinking about the familiar world, can and does slip into figuration, that usually unconscious activity by which sensation is figured into the familiar world of appearances. The once-conscious activity, which defines original participation, becomes unconscious but not inactive. The form and character of the world takes on the shape of that activity. In this sense do theories end up being perceived, appearing as an aspect of the familiar world. This is what it means to say the familiar world is correlative to consciousness. On the other hand, changing descriptions of the world—changes in the appearances—signal change in consciousness, the evolution of consciousness. The nexus between the two is figuration.

Another way to put this relation between figuration, consciousness, and the familiar world, is in terms of "conception" and "perception," "concepts" and "percepts." Conception is the activity of giving form to percepts, which of their own do not have any form or figure, demonstrated in the chapter on the first part of Barfield's *Saving the Appearances*. Perception is the initial and unconceptualized awareness of environmental stimuli. Conception, or thinking, gives form to percepts, or sensations. In Barfield's terms, sensations are figured into the objects of the everyday, familiar world. Figuration is a type of thinking, of conception, which is usually but not necessarily an unconscious process.

The degree to which perception is figured by concepts, by thinking, can vary. There can be perception heavily laced with conception, and there can be perception only minimally taken up in conception. Contemporary examples of the two extremes—maximal conceptualization/minimal perception, and minimal conception/maximal perception—would look like this: Two individuals are hiking through a mountain meadow. One of the individuals is a botanist and gardener. Every leaf, every flower and grass, tree, shrub, seed, moss and lichen, has a name, a color, relations to the other members of their communities. They each grow their special cycles, and reproduce and scatter in their particular ways. The botanist sees all this—the botanist *sees all of this.*

The other individual cannot tell a daisy from an aster, moss from green felt, bear grass from crab grass. The meadow is a vague carpet of patchy color, patches of light and dark—oh! There's a pine tree of some sort. For the one, conception informs practically every bit of the appearances, of the familiar world. For the other, almost bare percepts dominate the appearances, because conceptualization hardly touches them.

This contrast is evident in two different individuals in the same place at the same time. Now imagine this difference as a function of time, of history. Over time, two things change. One is the degree to which perception is figured by conception. The other is the awareness of the locus of the activity of conception. Barfield argues that, over time, conception has increased in proportion to perception, and the locus of the activity has shifted from being experienced independent of, but not always separate from, any one individual, to being experienced almost exclusively within oneself. Etymology—the history of the changing meaning of words—bears the burden of this conclusion. The older a human text, the more figurative—the more perceptual—the language is. Language today presents as highly abstract and conceptual. These same texts indicate that their authors found the activity of the figuring, the shaping, of appearances taking place outside themselves, outside their deliberate and conscious control, *but well within their awareness*. They were conscious of that activity taking place.

Today, the usual situation is that an individual regards the appearances as wholly independent of their awareness. They are just there. If there is any figuration, the individual is not aware of it. But if that individual *were* aware of it, where would they find it? As the nexus between that which is on the other side of the representations, the appearances, and the percipient, where would the percipient find the activity of figuration? Within themselves.

But where in themselves? As what? Samuel Taylor Coleridge talked about the activity of figuration, and located it within the individual. He called it imagination. He further noted two levels of imagination, which he called simply primary and secondary imagination. Secondary imagination is the sort exercised by poets and painters, who represent the appearances according to their will, their intentions and goals. This imagination is well within the control of the poet and painter. Primary imagination, Coleridge said, was the same sort of activity as secondary imagination, where perceptions are shaped and articulated, except that this activity was mostly unconscious, and the product of the process was not a poem or a landscape painting, but the very appearances of the world.

Taking imagination in this sense, together with Barfield's contention that the nature of imagination—of conscious figuration—has changed over time, then the difference in the basic nature of ancient and modern art as practice lies in the purported relation of the artist to the activity of the artist's creating. If imagination is the nexus between percept and concept, and if the proportion of the one to the other changes, as well as does the apparent locus of the activity, then for a Greek sculptor or medieval painter, the degree of controlled conception experienced as within the sculptor or painter was quite different from that of the Romantic poet or painter. What distinguishes ancient or medieval inspiration from

Romantic imaginative genius is the degree of conscious, deliberate, controlled conceptualization. And this is evident in the change in the very meaning of the words imagination and genius.

The nexus includes the use of language, especially what would be called poetic diction. It is under the control of the poet, whereby perception is infused with concepts by the poet's imagination. But this poetic imagination is of the same quality as that activity of conception which figures the world, the appearances, the ground one walks on and the air one breathes. In fact, to the degree that one is conscious of the latter activity, is one a co-creator of the product of that activity, namely, reality.

Now the connection between this purported history of imagination, and the history of philosophy, needs to be considered. As it turns out, Samuel Taylor Coleridge was quite smitten with the Kantian philosophy, even to the point of traveling to Germany to learn German and read Kant. Within Kant's philosophy, as Coleridge saw it, was an explicit description of such a relation between appearance, imagination, and the represented, as described above.

In the eighteenth century Immanuel Kant wrote his *Critique of Pure Reason*[cxxix] in which imagination is defined as an activity necessary to the unfolding of a familiar world. For Kant (as Barfield described in different terms), the unfolding of a phenomenal world was a rather complex process, once one assumed a reality composed of what Kant termed things-in-themselves (which Barfield called the unrepresented), which were independent of, and not apprehensible by, human consciousness. The complex process involved sensibility, imagination, and understanding—roughly corresponding to Barfield's represented, figuration, and beta-thinking. Knowledge was Kant's main concern, which was an awareness or experience of objects, spatial and/or temporal phenomena that are further articulated according to concepts. Or, knowledge was founded on sensible intuition synthesized according to the categories of the understanding.

Kant's focus on the nature and validity of knowledge was partly due to the work of the English philosopher David Hume. In his *Treatise of Human Nature,* Hume threw indubitable knowledge of the world into doubt by showing that relations such as the relation of causation—that A causes B—are merely inferred from experience and not necessary to or inherent in experience, in the objects external to the percipient. He argued instead that it was merely out of habit that one expected B to always follow A. The only certain knowledge was of mathematical and geometrical character, since it did not depend on perception of distinct events. But at the same time, and by definition, mathematical knowledge was worthless when it came to extending our knowledge of the natural world—the phenomena. Human certainty of the nature of reality was on shaky ground.

In response, Kant agreed that the connection between A and B was to be found in consciousness, in the perceiver, but not the way Hume meant. Kant went on to say that humans *can* know certainly and necessarily something about the world, namely, in what form the world will appear to us. In particular, one can know in advance of any perception whatsoever, just how—in what form and relations—those perceptions will appear to us. How can one know this in advance and for certain? Because it is by virtue of the nature of human consciousness itself that the appearances have this feature. "Yes," Kant said to Hume, "yes, causation doesn't exist out there with the A and the B in the same way that the A and the B exist. And yes, in a sense the relation of causation is a function of the constitution of the percipient. But due to that very fact, one can have certain knowledge of the shape so to speak, of any and all appearances, before one even sees them, because one has immediate intuition of this constitution. One cannot know *what* exactly will be experienced, but one can be certain *how* it will appear."

To really make this whole system plausible, though, Kant had to assume a number of other facts, three of which concern us here. One was that the human constitution, consciousness, had a definite and knowable form, and acted in definite and regular ways. Another was that human consciousness did not change. The third fact that Kant assumed: Though the very nature of human consciousness determines the nature of the appearances, that does not mean that fundamental reality is a function of human consciousness. Why? Because, independent of the world of appearances was the world of things-in-themselves. There was still the bedrock of objective reality unaltered by human thinking and concepts. So what is that independent reality doing out there? Kant argued that these things-in-themselves gave rise to intuition in a person via sensibility. This process of intuition, itself a mediation between things-in-themselves and human consciousness, is mediated by imagination, which Kant described as "a blind but indispensable function of the soul."[cxxx] In his terms, imagination synthesized the manifold of intuition. This synthesis is necessary for knowledge; the manifold must be "gone through in a certain way, taken up, and connected. This act I name synthesis."[cxxxi] Synthesis "is the mere result of the power of imagination."[cxxxii] Though blind, imagination is indispensable in the process of a phenomenal world arising from the interaction of human soul with things-in-themselves, including our-selves.

Kant suggested that it may seem the categories ought to be able to be applied to some kind of intuition that is non-sensible, such that one could directly experience things-in-themselves, which are non-sensible. One ought to be able to get a clear picture of things-in-themselves without the obfuscating media of sensibility and imagination. Such an object, supposed not to be an object of sensible intuition, Kant called noumenon.[cxxxiii] But when one thinks of the possibility of such a noumenon, "we thereby presuppose a special mode of intuition, namely, the intellectual, which is not that which we possess, and of which we cannot comprehend even the possibility."[cxxxiv]

So Kant examined and detailed human involvement in the phenomena, while at the same time demonstrated the independence of the things-in-themselves from human spontaneity. For an evolution of consciousness, this is the epitome of a philosophical doctrine of idolatry, because the appearances tell us nothing of things-in-themselves. At the same time there is in the *Critique*, for the evolutionist of consciousness, a quite sophisticated doctrine of final participation, for the phenomena are representational of human consciousness. Humans do participate in the phenomena, but not as the ancients or medievals did. Kant showed clearly the human un-connectedness from the unrepresented, but put human consciousness squarely in touch with the represented.

Kant's *Critique* gave a picture of, and feel for, the beginning of a textured and differentiated experience—a substantive experience—of self; *Kant sketched out the new-born self-consciousness.*[cxxxii] Insofar as things-in-themselves are beyond representation, there is no *original* participation, no immediacy of the represented (there is now an unrepresented), and the form of human consciousness is all that can be known. At the same time, since imagination is blind—one cannot be aware of its primary activity, which is to figure intuition into the appearances of the familiar world— human eyes have been fixed on the phenomena ever since, and thus idolatry, neat and crisp, begins it star-studded career.

In the end Kant sowed the seed of the notion of a new kind of participation, for though humans seem mesmerized by the phenomena, it is consciousness that constitutes those phenomena. Barfield argued that once we accept things-in-themselves, then we must accept the everyday world as a system of collective representations, and further, that if the collective representations of the ancients and medievals and primitives are different from our present-day representations, then it only makes sense to say that they lived in a different world from our own.

II

In contemporary philosophy, the notion of figuring a different world is known under the name "alternative conceptual frameworks." Richard Rorty says, "the notion of alternative conceptual frameworks has been a commonplace of our culture since Hegel."[cxxxvi] Rorty also regards Kant to have contributed to this cultural heritage:

> Hegel's' historicism gave us a sense of how there might be genuine novelty in the development of thought and of society. Such a historicist conception of thought and morals was, we may see by hindsight, rendered possible by Kant...[cxxxvii]

It is in this vein that contemporary philosophy engages Barfield most directly, and actually by name, as seen later in this chapter. Philosophy restricts this engagement to occasional remarks and references, yet the details of the issues common to Barfield's evolution of consciousness and philosophy's alternative conceptual frameworks justify accepting some of the objections to the latter as applicable to the former.

An essential implication of Barfield's analysis of the contemporary reality principle bequeathed to the West as the scientific world view, is that the world before the scientific revolution was a different world from the world since that revolution. Central to Barfield's treatment, in turn, is the Kantian characterization of the nature of reality: there are the appearances, which correspond in form to consciousness, and then there are the noumena, to which the human mind and senses have absolutely no access. What the human mind shapes are intuitions, originating in the noumena, yes, but in no way representative of the noumena. That shaping, which Kant calls synthesis, is the activity of human imagination according to certain rules or schemes or categories, which Kant actually enumerated.

As stated in the previous section, Kant assumed a number of things about this whole system he articulated. One of them was that this scheme of categories was universal, it was the basic character of consciousness as consciousness. He not only assumed it to be universal, but also unchanging over time. This premise is less explicit than the first. Yet the categories themselves, for instance, are little different from the categories that Aristotle enumerated thousands of years before.

How can a Kantian metaphysic in any way be construed as the basis of its opposite, namely, a metaphysic according to which categories vary from time to time and from place to place? Remember that the synthesis of intuitions according to a set of categories or concepts—according to a conceptual scheme—accounts for the character of the appearances of reality. The implication of this latter metaphysic is that there are different appearances for different conceptual schemes. There is the one world, but the categories that determine the character of the appearance of reality differ between peoples, and between eras.

This seeming conjurers trick is made possible by Kant primarily in the suggestion that there is some fundamental slippage or gap between the underlying and unchanging reality—the things-in-themselves which are untouched by consciousness—and the appearances of the everyday world. Kant articulates this initially general hypothesis into great detail on the side of human consciousness. The sheer volume of words and earnestness of arguments expended in this articulation are almost enough by themselves to convince the reader of Kant's *Critique of Pure Reason* that this is the way reality is.

But this gap between the two halves of reality, noumena and phenomena, is only one of several distinct features of Kant's metaphysic, and not every feature was grasped and granted as fully as this one feature. The whole schematic construct of consciousness was nearly as fully granted and assumed after time. What was not as fully accepted were the universal and unchanging qualities of this construct. It was perhaps only a matter of time before a fully convinced Kantian in regard to the "gap and schematic" features begins to directly question the "universal and unchanging" features. Richard Rorty's statement above regarding Hegel points to one of the first and influential philosophers to do so.

The historic result is a tradition of thought that accepts that human consciousness is as essential in accounting for the character of the appearances of the everyday world as is an underlying and unrepresented substance or world. Hegel was especially tuned to the developmental and dialectical nature of thought and thinking. His philosophy of history was as much a history of human consciousness, and strongly suggested the changing nature of the appearances as a correlative. There was still the underlying world, but there were also these different and changing syntheses of the intuitions to which that world gives rise.

That is why Richard Rorty sees Hegel and Kant the two most important players in the development of the notion of alternative conceptual schemes. That is why his criticism of this notion involves arguments against Kant's metaphysic. Insofar as Barfield's starting point in *Saving the Appearances* was a popularized Kantian metaphysic, then Rorty's criticisms of the notion of alternative conceptual schemes may be generalized to criticisms of an evolution of consciousness.

What is Rorty's argument? Primarily, Rorty finds unintelligible the notion of an underlying and independent world, the noumena, which goes hand in hand with the alternative conceptual schemes to produce different worlds. Rorty determines this world to be neutral material, or "Kantian unsynthesized intuition."[cxxxviii] Rorty points out that if Kantian neutral material really is neutral, then it cannot, in any explicable way, determine how it will be synthesized. On the other hand, if it is not neutral, if it does to some degree determine how consciousness synthesizes it, then it is no longer completely unrepresented, it is no longer noumenal. So if the unsynthesized intuition really is unsynthesized, then it is also ineffable, since language is based on the structure of the categories of consciousness (Aristotle's categories applied explicitly to language). If it is ineffable, then it "is incapable of having an explanatory function."[cxxxix]

Once this intuition is spoken, continues Rorty, then it has been synthesized—how else could one put it into words? Therefore it is not
really independent of human consciousness. In order to make sense of a
phrase like alternative conceptual schemes, Rorty argues, one must be
able to distinguish and identify what is being shaped, and the shaping
power or function itself. How else can one make sense of the statement
that the world can be shaped in different ways? Rorty enlists another
philosopher, Donald Davidson[cxl] to argue this point, that the distinction between content and scheme—what is ordered or organized, and
the system according to which it is ordered—cannot be made in a
coherent way.

Rorty and Davidson take up with proponents of the notion of alternative conceptual schemes who suggest that such schemes are recognizable in
differences of language. Barfield certainly falls into this category: the
nature of human consciousness is evident in texts, and those texts show a
marked change from their first beginnings to the texts of today. Davidson
and Rorty argue that what is necessary for this argument is some way of
distinguishing between differences in language due to different schemes—
and therefore different worlds—on the one hand, and differing points of
view of one and the same world on the other. The question becomes, How
do we distinguish between qualitative and quantitative differences? In
order to unpack this issue, Davidson suggests that an example of an
extreme quantitative difference ought to provide a nice practice problem.

Consider a language spoken by aliens, a language to which humans are
wholly unsuccessful in correlating an environment, a world. This might be
due to their profoundly different conceptual scheme, such that the way
they take up with the world does not at all coincide with the way humans
take up with the world. But in this case, say Davidson and Rorty, is there
any reason then to call the vocal behavior of those aliens a language at all?
They might as well be regarded as not having any language whatsoever, as
is assumed of stones and rivers, butterflies and trees, since the sounds they
emit cannot be correlated to anything in phenomena present to humans.

Alternatively, if a translation is more or less successful, that is, if a correlation of vocal behavior with environment is more or less successful, is there any reason to conclude anything more spectacular than a slight difference in perspective, as opposed to a different conceptual scheme? In this example, an alternative conceptual scheme is indistinguishable from what is already and uncontroversially called a different point of view of one world.

The world, then, says Rorty, is either vacuous, as seen in the discussion of the Kantian unsynthesized intuition, or it is what was always thought— the world is the collection of those things that all agree exist, that are not questioned, that are taken for granted, with only slight differences which are called differences in opinion, or something else equally uninteresting. The only intelligible statement in this regard is that humans are in touch with the world most of the time, for facts in dispute are few, relative to the other ones that are not. Rorty goes on to say that insofar as the nature of the world is taken to be the arbiter between the "noncompeting trivialities"[cxli] of idealism and realism, then any attempt to define the world, beyond it being "those planks in the boat which are at the moment not being moved about,"[cxlii] is a mad, pathological chase. He suggests that philosophers can "stop doing philosophy,"[cxliii] if such is philosophy, and can instead attempt to "solve problems—to modify our beliefs and desires and activities in ways that will bring us greater happiness than we have now."[cxliv] Let us consider Rorty's alternative in more detail.

In his essays "The Contingency of Language" and "The Contingency of Selfhood"[cxlv] Rorty attempts, as the only intelligible task for philosophy, what he set out in the last paragraph of "The World Well Lost":

> [N]ow that these criticisms [of Kantian epistemology] have taken hold, the time may have come to try to recapture Dewey's "naturalized" version of Hegelian historicism. In this historicist vision, the arts, the sciences, the sense of right and wrong, and the institutions of society are not attempts to embody or formulate truth or

goodness or beauty. They are attempts to solve problems—to modify our beliefs and desires and activities in ways that will bring us greater happiness than we have now.[cxlvi]

Rorty tells new stories, stories in which the world of Kantian things-in-themselves is "de-divinise[d]."[cxlvii] Contingency, and not neutral material or The World, is the stuff of life. Language and self are not divine, but contingent, because science, poetry, and politics alike are metaphorical, are linguistic structures. Human nature is nothing neither more nor less than the language of our politics, poetry, and science. Rorty's reasoning is straightforward: human activity is to speak; to speak is to be; to speak differently is to be different. Further, truth is only where sentences are; and sentences are only where human language is, and "human languages are human creations."[cxlviii] Truth is a human creation, and does not refer to the status of the relationship between language and The World, which affirms or negates that language. Nor does this truth jive with idealism, if that idealism clings to "the very idea of anything—mind or matter, self or world—having an intrinsic nature to be expressed or represented."[cxlix] Truth, for Rorty, is a linguistic construct, and he urges us to see language "as we now see evolution—as new forms of life constantly killing off old forms."[cl]

Rorty continues his story, lest one holds onto some pathological dream of essence. He goes on to tell of an idiosyncratic "I," itself contingent, precluding personality as a last hideout for idealistic notions. Rorty enlists Harold Bloom, Friedrich Nietszche, and Sigmund Freud for the work of de-divinisation of the subject, the poet/politician/metaphysician, now that poetry and politics and metaphysics themselves are mortal and idiosyncratic and contingent. Rorty is forestalling the response that says, Even if there is no such thing as objectivity, there may yet be something called subjectivity, and it could have all the qualities of objectivity that the idealist holds sacred. But this is not to be; the subject is doomed to the same fate as the object.

Each person is distinct, and not merely "a copy or a replica."[cli] Distinction can be traced back, not to some universal and blind impress, but to chance, to "the contingencies of our upbringings."[clii] "I" am no instance of a species, but am "contingent relations, a web that stretches backward and forward through past and future time,"[cliii] a web which bears thus the impress of each individual's "project of self-creation through imposition of one's own idiosyncratic metaphoric."[cliv] The web grows each day. The project continues. New metaphors keep getting made, and old ones continue to die and add to the fabric of the web with their dead bodies. The free play of language that one sees today, in contrast to the orthodox, doctrinal, and magical attitudes of the past, Rorty says is due to the contingency of language—it is not fixed, neither in the world, nor in self as some expression of essence. Exactly like traditional evolution, the progress of language usage is due to nothing but chance.

In Rorty's latter two essays he denies the representational nature of anything, contra Barfield, and then he suggests the alternative of evolution, which is Barfield's alternative as well. How is Barfield's evolution of consciousness any different than Rorty's? Barfield too spoke of free play in language today, and pointed to the poetry of the Romantics as especially enlightening examples; and both Rorty and Barfield acknowledge the self-conscious character of the Romantic movement, as a movement to use language in a deliberately and seriously creative manner. Barfield saw the Romantics to have attempted to re-establish a representational nature of nature, but a nature representational not of what was on the other side of nature from themselves, but of what was on the other side of themselves from nature. The Romantics deliberately reinterpreted—experienced—nature as representational of the human being. The spirit behind nature was gone with the scientific revolution, but Barfield thought that there was more to it than that. Pan, it seems, has not only not retired from business;

he has not only gone indoors; he has hardly shut the door, before we hear him moving about inside.[clv]

For Romanticism

[i]t is no longer simply that the arts 'reascend to those principles from which nature herself is derived.' The 'principles' themselves have changed their venue. For we are told by the Romantic theory that we must no longer look for the nature-spirits—for the Goddess Natura—on the farther side of the appearances; we must look for them within ourselves.[clvi]

It is clear that though Barfield and Rorty deem romanticism as important to the discussion of the history of philosophy, they differ in their treatment of the Romantics: Rorty is critical, insofar as he treats their talk of representation as mistaken. Rorty admits of no human interior, nor exterior for that matter, as they go hand in hand, and depend on what he argues is a vacuous Kantian thing-in-itself—something not wholly present. Though Rorty does admit that one is not always present to or aware of the world, he accepts that absence as not interesting. For Rorty, though the Romantics did much to effect their own idiosyncratic metaphoric, they did so thinking that such language was expressive of something deeper. But they were wrong.

At this point a discussion of the notion of metaphor will be helpful, for two reasons. First, metaphor is the poetic tool par excellence. Aristotle spoke of the making of metaphor as the preeminent poetic art, and as something not able to be taught, though it could be described in terms of series of associations. As the poetic construct, it is understood as the representational construct as well. So a look at such a construct will show us in fine what Barfield and Rorty take to be the nature of representation.

Second, metaphor will be helpfully discussed because on this score one finds the most direct connection between Barfield's work and Rorty. Donald Davidson's work on metaphor will he helpful, because Rorty acknowledges often his debt to Davidson in this vein, and because Davidson refers directly to Barfield. Mainstream philosophy meets Barfield directly, and the engagement can instruct the present discussion. In his essay "What Metaphors Mean,"[clvii] Davidson argues that a metaphor—which can be considered as central to the Romantic poetry, in practice and theory—is not a vehicle of some hidden meaning, some interior truth, but that they mean what the words literally denote. The significance of metaphoric utterance is instead due to their effect: they draw our attention to something. In order to discourage one from thinking that there is some formal and regular—causal—relation between the metaphor and that to which it draws attention, Davidson likens the effect to being hit on the head with a hammer, and one may then see any number of things. Davidson quotes an essay by Barfield, "Poetic Diction and Legal Fiction,"[clviii] in which Barfield stated that a metaphor "says one thing and means another."[clix] Davidson says, in short, 'No, Barfield has confused the effect of a metaphor with a supposed "hidden meaning" of a metaphor.'

There is no fundamental disagreement between Barfield and Davidson, if Barfield's "a metaphor says one thing and means another" is understood as a metaphor literally says one thing, and points us to another thing. This is entirely consistent with his understanding of meaning. Barfield saw the evolution of consciousness, from one perspective, as a progression from an immediate awareness of the meaning of phenomena, to a preoccupation with the phenomena themselves. Final participation is the practice of a new link with that meaning. To have one's attention directed, by literal denotation, to some other thing, only precludes Barfield's understanding of metaphor if things do not mean. For Barfield they did.

Further, Barfield himself was convinced that a metaphor does in fact do something. In *Poetic Diction* Barfield premised that work on the fact that a metaphor does something, namely, it induces a "felt change of consciousness,"[clx] which is certainly consistent with Davidson's hammer blow to the head. What Barfield meant in particular by a felt change of consciousness was a change from normal consciousness—normal for oneself—to a different consciousness—consciousness experienced as different.

It is at this point that the reader of Barfield encounters the difference between his theory of metaphor and that of much of contemporary thought, represented by Davidson: Barfield argued that that different consciousness which was induced by the metaphor was somehow akin to the consciousness that produced or inspired the creation of the metaphor. This is not to suggest any lexicon of metaphor where metaphors are lined up with their particular and unique and detailed essences. But Barfield did suggest a regular connection between true metaphor—that which imparts knowledge—and the consciousness that produced it. Davidson's distinction between the meaning and the effect of a metaphor is a helpful one, if it serves to clarify and enrich, rather than preclude, Barfield's notion: metaphors are like hammers put to heads, in that one experiences a felt change of consciousness when engaged with that metaphor. Barfield assumed that meaning is not parceled out into discrete quanta, but involved or implicated the whole of consciousness. Therefore, the content of that different consciousness, whatever that content may be, is the meaning of the metaphor.

Barfield was convinced of the present free play of language and meaning, but he did not agree that it was due merely to chance, nor did he imply that all of the history of philosophy before Wittgenstein was a sham and a mistake, as Richard Rorty seems to. Barfield took issue with the role and nature of chance to begin with. Chance is not implicit in evolution itself. This is the essential difference between Darwinian evolution and an evolution of consciousness. Insofar as Barfield's evolution of consciousness was meant to save the appearances of changes in meanings evident in human texts, it is an hypothesis, as all hypotheses are meant to save the appearances of some kind. In this sense, though, "the concept of chance is precisely what a hypothesis is devised to save us from. Chance, in fact, = no hypothesis."[clxi] Chance cannot be analyzed, and therefore is no help whatever in making human history intelligible. Whereas the "forces at work beneath the threshold of argument in the evolution...of...consciousness" can be, if not analyzed, at least enumerated, described, and related to.

In the scheme of an evolution of consciousness, individuals are now able to use language—as Rorty too argues, but from different premises. According to Barfield, such free play was not evident in the mythic language of the oldest texts. Meaning in this period was given. What Rorty says about the given being a myth, Barfield turned on its head: Myth, the meaning of myth, was given. Meaning is no longer given, not because it was a lie or mistake from the beginning, but because things have changed—consciousness has evolved.

Barfield showed that a Kantian metaphysic is as good a diagnosis of the Western state of mind as any, and the more intelligible. But Barfield, unlike for Kant, granted that imagination need not be blind. If the appearances—which is all there is to the reality commonly regarded—are to be saved, it will only be so if imagination can see. In Kantian terms, the thing-in-itself, as out there, is not accessible, but the phenomenal manifold, which is synthesized by the imagination, is accessible. In this scheme, Richard Rorty's attack on Kant's thing-in-itself does not apply to a Kantian manifold. And it is the relation between such a manifold and imagination that is the crux of Barfield's work in *Saving the Appearances*.

Even the Kantian thing-in-itself may not be so inaccessible as all that.[clxii] Though Kant introduced the purely limiting concept of noumenon, as an object of insensible intuition, it was for him purely limiting because he could not "comprehend even the possibility." Kant argued the limits of our sensibility, our intuition, as a limit to our knowledge, our conceptualizing. Rorty argued that Kantianism is pathology, and suggested his pragmatic philosophy as therapeutic, not in the sense of fixing Kantianism, but by avoiding it like the plague. Chance is worthy of our respect as the shaper of language and selves. There is no stuff out there somewhere, whether inside or out, that somehow one shapes.

On the other hand, if consciousness has evolved, then Kant, Kantianism, and Rorty's pragmatism are not simply mutually exclusive alternatives. They have told parts of a powerful story, but parts which, if told apart from a redemptive myth such as Barfield's, simply lose their power as edifying stories because they fail to tell us why such edification is really necessary. Rorty—and Davidson and Nietszche and Wittgenstein—have helped further break the attachment to language, extending the de-divinisation process to language. Insofar as those linguistic representations are idolatrous, which ironically Rorty supposes to de-divinise, then Rorty's arguments imply the possibility of speaking a Kantian language without being attached to the meanings—the phenomena—to which Kant himself was attached when speaking as he did. But unless one is convinced of the seriousness of the detachment from the world which Kant articulated, then attachment—or edification—is merely idiosyncratic metaphoric. In light of an evolution of consciousness, on the other hand, the history of philosophy turns out to be an ongoing experience with the manifold itself, and out of that, an evolving dialogue with oneself. Edification becomes redemption, and the result is to reveal the true significance of one's conversation, and one's life.

The next to last chapter presents moments in that ongoing experience with the manifold, moments in an evolution of consciousness approached in the traditional texts of philosophy. At the very least, it will be evident whether or not such engagements, in the light of the evolution of consciousness, look any different than a merely dialectical history of thought. It will also suggest whether or not Barfield's work is capable of informing a different look at the history of western thinking.

The Impossibility of
Interpenetration as the Problem
of the Other

Underlying the claim that the history of language shows indications of the evolution of consciousness is the assumption that via language a consciousness unlike one's own can be directly experienced. The assumption is stated explicitly in *Poetic Diction*, and is implicit in Barfield's discussion of the mind of the Greeks and Romans, and the medieval worldview in *Saving the Appearances*. This assumption is clearly a scandal in western philosophy at least since Descartes, but even before that, when Galileo proposed the distinction between occult and non-occult qualities in nature. John Locke distinguished the primary and secondary qualities, where the latter, such as color, warmth, and taste were subjective experiences of the observer, and the former, including extension and mass, were inherent in the objects themselves. If one wanted to know the truth about the external world, then the secondary qualities must be distinguished from the primary, so as not to obfuscate one's view of the latter.

It may seem odd, or simply untrue, that philosophy takes this view, that the subjective qualities of the world are to be distinguished from the objective facts in order to know the truth about the facts, since it is philosophy that is ostensibly carrying on the tradition of Socrates:

Know thyself. Further, philosophy deals with the mind, with ideas and concepts, and what are they if not subjective? For the most part, though, whether one is an idealist or a realist, an empiricist or a rationalist, attention is given to ideas and concepts *as end products*. Much less attention is given, if at all, to the activity that creates these end products. Even phenomenology, the science of consciousness, deals more with the static structures of consciousness, rather than an activity, and certainly not as an evolving activity. In fact, phenomenology tends to be much more like, and often is, logical analysis, than it is anything like Barfield's historical experience of language.

Nonetheless, phenomenology, as the science of consciousness, does take up with issues germane to Barfield's evolution of consciousness. It is in works of phenomenology that one finds discussions most like Barfield's *Saving the Appearances*. Specifically, it is in phenomenology that one finds a whole host of work regarding the experience of other human beings: the details of encounters, and attempts at describing an underlying ontology that makes intelligible those encounters. One such work, Jean Paul Sartre's *Being and Nothingness,* is an exceptional instance of this phenomenology of the other, and will be discussed in this chapter.

Sartre's work recommends itself for another, and very important, reason: the descriptions he offers of the encounter with the other, and his ontology meant to explain the nature of such encounters, is in many details very like a similar exercise by another philosopher who is closely allied with Barfield. This philosopher is Rudolf Steiner, and his work is *The Philosophy of Freedom.* In the first section, then, the work of Sartre and Steiner will be compared, and the reader will see two very different answers to the question: Can one experience the consciousness of another? Having been introduced to Steiner's thought, in the following section we will then explore his thought more deeply, see what light it sheds on Barfield's own work. For, from the beginning of Barfield's career as a philosopher to the time of his death, he never tired of acknowledging his deep debt to the life and writings of Rudolf Steiner.

The Other

Part Three of Jean-Paul Sartre's *Being and Nothingness*[clxiii] is entitled "Being-for-Others," the first chapter of which is entitled "The Existence of Others." But he introduces us to this section in the last paragraph of the preceding Part Two:

> Perhaps some may be surprised that we have treated the problem of knowing without raising the question of the body and the senses or even once referring to it. It is not my purpose to misunderstand or ignore the role of the body. But what is important above all else, in ontology as elsewhere, is to observe strict order in discussion. Now the body, whatever may be its function, appears first as the known. We can not therefore refer knowledge back to it or discuss it before we have defined knowing, nor can we derive knowledge in its fundamental structure from the body in any way or manner whatsoever. Furthermore the body—our body—has for its peculiar characteristic the fact that it is essentially that which is known by the Other. What I know is the body of another, and the essential facts which I know concerning my own body come from the way in which others see it. Thus the nature of my body refers me to the existence of others and to my being-for-others. I discover with it for human reality another mode of existence as fundamental as being-for-itself, and this I shall call being-for-others.[clxiv]

Thus it is in consideration of the body that we find and describe what is for Sartre a third mode of being, beside being-in-itself and being-for-itself.

Sartre shows revealed the fundamental being-for-others, and thus the Other, by making explicit the difference between internal and external negation, and showing that the Other and the for-itself, i.e., consciousness, internally constitute one another's being. He asserts that the Other's existence cannot be proved, but only encountered; and any cogitation on the matter is movement to such an encounter.

> Thus we must ask the For-itself to deliver to us the For-others; we must ask absolute immanence to throw us into absolute transcendence. In my inmost depths I must find not reasons for believing that the Other exists but the Other [itself] as not being me.[clxv]

The detail of this Other will be articulated in internal negation, "a synthetic, active connection of the two terms, each one of which constitutes itself by denying that it is the other."[clxvi] Further, this internal negation will reveal, not an object, but a for-itself like mine. Thus does Sartre discuss, and at length (60 pages), "The Look" in which I am constituted as an object—a body—by a subject.

This revelation of the Other as a subject and not as an object marks the difference between "a primary relation between my consciousness and the Other's,"[clxvii] on the one hand, and the "purely conjectural"[clxviii] existence of an Other on the other hand.

> This relation, in which the Other must be given to me directly as a subject although in connection with me, is the fundamental relation, the very type of my being-for-others.[clxix]

Appropriately Sartre next asks, Where and when do we encounter this Other? He answers,

> It is in the reality of everyday life that the Other appears to us...In order to understand [the original relation to the

Other] I must question more exactly this ordinary appearance of the Other in the field of my perception; since this appearance refers to that fundamental relation, the appearance must be capable of revealing to us, at least as a reality aimed at, the relation to which it refers.[clxx]

Consistent with that proposal, he begins, "I am in a public park."[clxxi] This gets us to the heart of what I see as the value of Sartre's ontology in a study of Otherness: his delicate descriptions of one's perceptual field which phenomenology has made its primary concern. I will therefore quote at some length in order to 'get a feel' for this valuable descripting.

I see [a] man; I apprehend him as an object and at the same time as a man...If I were to think of him as only being a puppet, [only an object,]...no new relation would appear through him between those things [—the benches, the trees, the grass—] in my universe...Perceiving him as a man, on the other hand...is to register an organization without distance of the things in my universe around that privileged object...[T]he distance is unfolded starting from the man whom I see and extending up to the lawn as the synthetic upsurge of a universal relation. We are dealing with a relation which is without parts, given at one stroke, inside of which there unfolds a spatiality which is not my spatiality; for instead of a grouping toward me of the objects, there is now an orientation which flees from me...[and] if there exists between the lawn and the Other a relation which is without distance and which creates distance, then there exists necessarily a relation between the Other and the statue which stands on a pedestal in the middle of the lawn...[T]here is total space which is grouped around the Other, and this space is made with my space; there is a regrouping in which I take part but which escapes me, a regrouping of all the objects which people my universe...[I]t appears that the world has a kind of drainhole in the middle of its being and that it is perpetually flowing off through this hole.[clxxii]

So far, though, for all this collapse of the universe into a thick, syrupy liquid draining around some drainhole, we have mot encountered more that a unique object, says Sartre; we have not encountered a subject. It is probable that a subject 'lies behind the eyes that look,' but we want a revelation, not a probability. But that probability can help us to go on further, to where we can 'bump into' the Other, because the apprehension of an object "as probably being a man refers to my permanent possibility of being-seen-by-him."[clxxiii] That "internal hemorrhage" of being is the pull of the Other on it—the look of the Other that shifts the world's—my world's—orientation; and I myself can be looked at, too, just as the lawn and the trees and the benches can be looked at. I too can become an object. If I do, I cannot be so for another object, an object of the world, "since I am precisely the one by whom there is a world; that is, the one who on principle cannot be an object for himself."

> Thus this relation which I call 'being-seen-by-another,' far from being merely one of the relations signified by the word man, represents an irreducible fact which can not be deduced either from the essence of the Other-as-object, or from my being-as-subject.[clxxiv]

We have bumped into the Other.

Next Sartre asks, If this Other is the one who looks at me, the one by whom I am seen, then what is that look? The look of the Other is not an object in my world—it is not a pair of eyes in the sockets of a head. In fact, the look of the Other "hides his eyes; he seems to go in front of them.

This illusion stems from the fact that eyes as objects of my perception remain at a precise distance which unfolds from me to them...whereas the look is upon me without distance while at the same time it holds me at a distance.[clxxv]

When I attend to the look, "at the same stroke [I cause] my perception to decompose and pass into the background."[clxxvi] Thus "when I hear branches crackling behind me" I do not apprehend "that there is someone there,"[clxxvii] but rather, 'I am here!' My perception immediately collapses as I apprehend "that I have a body," a body "which can be hurt" and is vulnerable.[clxxviii] What does the look mean, then? "It means that I am suddenly affected in my being and that essential modifications appear in my structure."[clxxixi]

Interpenetration: Bad Faith, or Good Phenomenology?

The goal of this chapter is to show us a way to the very nexus of our bond with the Other in wildness, in the body of feelings, as interpenetration of Self with Other, consciousness with consciousness. Sartre himself was far from acknowledging any such co-(mm)-union amongst Self and Other. In fact, he flatly denies it.

> It is...useless for human reality to seek to get out of this dilemma: one must either transcend the Other [that is, make them your object,] or allow oneself to be transcended by him. The essence of the relations between consciousnesses is not the Mitsein [of Heidegger]; it is conflict.[clxxx]

The conflict that Sartre posits is between consciousnesses. By the very definition of consciousness as intentional, as a being for, Sartre consistently draws out the most profound consequences for human reality, namely, freedom. That freedom is the heart of the nothingness that is consciousness. Freedom is that we are, in our essence, nothing—we have no essence. To be conscious is to be conscious of, and thus nothing can 'stick' to us: we can always nihilate the being of what we are. I can be conscious of my cowardice, for instance, but by the very activity of being conscious of it, then 'it' is 'there,' and 'I' am 'here.' 'I' am not 'it' once I reflect on it. I cannot even apprehend myself except as a nothingness; I flee myself. Thus would a consciousness be that is not my own: it is not me. As consciousness I am always a flight.

This is the reason for the ever present possibility of bad faith, the multitudinous attempts on our part to settle into Being-in-itself that simply is. We want to be, and to be free; but for Sartre, to be freedom is the nihilating activity that is consciousness; freedom posits an in-itself that is not consciousness, that is not freedom. We attempt to collapse into Being-in-itself, as a freedom, and this is impossible. We attempt to identify—to exactly match, to cram ourselves into without remainder—our (admirable or shameful) past deeds which simply are. But if we succeeded, then we would fail to be conscious of it, to know it, to experience it—we could only be it. If we do not succeed, then we must affirm our freedom, our not being our past. Or we may try to affirm only our freedom, our nihilating activity of consciousness, in order to escape identification with our past. But this involves affirmation of exactly what we deny, what we wish to not be. For to say "I am freedom" is again to try to collapse into the in-itself, to not be that freedom.

Consciousness flees, flees even being, even itself; attempts to do otherwise lead inevitably to failure. In relation to Others the story is the same: I attempt either to 'maintain' my freedom as subject, and thus make the Other an object; or I can 'allow' my own objectivation by the Other's subjectivity, but both are failures to penetrate the consciousness of the Other, for in the first instance the Other is an object and not a consciousness; in the other instance I am the object.

Sartre has bound us with his own Cartesian ontology, and it does not look promising. Whether of Sartrean origin or not, this same bind is common enough in, for example, discussions of wilderness issues in which 'anthropocentrist' may be as nasty a name for an environmentalist to call someone as 'patriarch' is for a feminist, or 'devil worshipper' for the fundamentalist. Taking the gross lack of self-conscious articulation of the term as license to suggest my own sense, the term means "a human who supposes any aspect of their own experience to validly obtain for a non-human." Usually these aspects are mental, emotional, or ethical, and to maintain the charge usually involves varieties of the hapless dynamic Sartre so aptly describes in sado-masochistic terms: humans either are the inert 'things' absolutely defined by their thing-like, unchanging character (usually greedy, wasteful, power-hungry, arrogant, etc.) while the natural, non-human world is absolutely spontaneous and free-flowing; or humans are shiftless beings condemned to unabated and restless flight and fancy, while non-human nature reposes in the fund of heavy, ponderous, thick, wonderful, unchanging (or very, very, very slowly changing) Being.

I have two responses here. First, as to Sartre: the phenomenological, synthetic/perceptual descriptions of the world of objects in our daily lives I think a real treasure and an example of a possibly therapeutic attitude that one may take in encountering a splintered world. Second, what he has described can well be considered from another viewpoint regarding the interpenetration of consciousnesses. I will address the latter first.

In *The Philosophy of Spiritual Activity* (*Philosophie der Freiheit*, 1894) Rudolf Steiner attempted to prove that

> there is a view concerning man's being which can support the rest of knowledge; and, further…to point out how with this view we gain a complete justification for the Idea of free will, provided only that we have first discovered that region of the soul in which free volition can unfold itself.[clxxxi]

The knowledge with which Steiner is concerned is not a Kantian a-historical, transcendent, unchanging "knowledge which has encased itself once and for all in frozen formulas."[clxxxii]

> The answer given to the problems [of knowledge and freedom] will not be of the purely theoretical sort...The book will not give a ready-made and conclusive answer of this sort, but point to a field of experience in which [one's] own inward soul activity supplies a living answer to these questions...Whoever has once discovered the region of the soul where these questions unfold, will find precisely in [their] actual acquaintance with this region all that [they need] for the solution of these two problems...Thus it would appear that there is a kind of knowledge which proves its justification and validity by its own inner life.[clxxxiii]

Steiner argues that there is a difference between "a conscious motive and an unconscious impulse of action,"[clxxxiv] and that this distinction is important to a treatment of freedom. Thus his question is, "[W]hat of the freedom of an action about the motives of which we know?"[clxxxv] This question "leads us to the question of the origin and meaning of thinking."[clxxxvi] Because of the relations of motive to action, and thinking to motive, "the question of the nature of human action presupposes that of the origin of thinking."[clxxxvii] He then argues that thinking itself must be "the instrument of knowledge,"[clxxxviii] for when thinking about thinking nothing heterogeneous—and therefore in need of further analysis—is added to thinking, as when one thinks about an object.

It will be helpful to draw out the relevance of this particular point to the above-mentioned discussion of wilderness and otherness. Specifically, in saying that anthropocentrism is an invalid and/or unjustifiable stance to take toward nature, the environmentalist usually posits some kind of ecocentrism or biocentrism. Either way, though, the difficulty does not magically disappear. Insofar as anthropocentrism is taken to be an invalid 'projection' of some aspect of human experience, the environmentalist may argue that non-human being does not experience as we humans do; at least, we cannot know that it does. But this begs the question of how we do experience the world, which is the very matter under discussion, and which cannot be prejudged. Even if we suppose that non-human being is not conscious as we are, any kind of bio- or eco-centric participation in the world on our human part will be a conscious activity in one way or another, and thus we have not escaped anthropocentrism, insofar as anthropocentrism involves human consciousness. If we argue that non-human being is conscious, then we are already participating in that being insofar as we are conscious. Thus it looks quite reasonable that thinking, which for Steiner is in part characterized by its intentionality as consciousness is for Sartre, should be included in our investigation.

Thus does Steiner begin his phenomenology of freedom. What is of particular interest for us is his description of interaction with others. In an appendix to *The Philosophy of Spiritual Activity* he addresses the question of "how one's own soul can be affected by another's."[clxxxix] He says that the problem only comes up because of certain prejudice in thinking, which leads to the formulation of this question:

> [T]he world of my consciousness is a closed circle within me; so is the world of another's consciousness within [them]. I cannot look into the world of another's consciousness. How, then, do I know that [they] and I are in a common world?"[cxc]

Steiner rehearses the Kantian argument that hypothesizes a noumenal world in order to avoid solipsism. Steiner rejects this view which puts "an artificial structure of concepts in front of reality,"[cxci] and instead describes the experience of encountering others.

What is it that, in the first instance, I have before me when I confront another person? To begin with, there is the sensuous appearance of the other's body, as given in perception.[cxcii]

Steiner has argued previously that 'the real' is perception—or percepts—"permeated" by conception—or concepts.

The percept, thus, is not something finished and self-contained, but one side of the total reality. The other side is the concept...only the percept and the concept together constitute the whole thing.[cxciii]

Further, perception "sets in motion"[cxciv] thinking activity, the latter being the connecting up of percepts with concepts. Percepts are "the immediate objects of sensation...insofar as the conscious subject apprehends them through observation."[cxcv] They are objective, contra Critical Idealism which argues that they are subjective, but on the basis of the Naive Realist assumption of their objectivity. That is, the idealist says that because our bodily organization relativizes the sensations, then they are mere appearances. Yet so, then, is the bodily constitution; and there goes the subjectivity of our perceptions. Thus what we perceive is objective, yet not real by itself. The concept is "an ideal element...added to the perceived object."[cxcvi] The whole of our perceptual field is "the world of appearances,"[cxcvii] and 'the real' is that region or regions of the field permeated by concepts, by thinking activity.

Steiner also argues that, contrary to common sense, it is percepts that mark us as individuals, and thinking or conception which is universal.

In so far as we sense and feel (and also perceive), we are single beings; in so far as we think, we are the All-One

Being which pervades everything...We see a simply absolute force revealing itself in us, which is universal. But we learn to know it, not as it issues from the centre of the world, but rather at a point of the periphery.[cxcviii]

This dualism is only such "from the moment that I as spectator confront things."[cxcix] Both thought and perception are part of an antecedent whole, which is split by our spectation. Percepts alone are not real; when we encounter the world as appearance—which, again, is objective—the whole is again constituted by adding what our physical organization cuts us off from in observation: thinking.

It follows for Steiner that our

psycho-physical organization...contributes nothing to the essential nature of thought, but recedes whenever the activity of thinking appears. It suspends its own activity, it yields ground. And the ground thus set free is occupied by thinking.[cc]

This explains what happens next in our encounter with another thinking consciousness.

Through the thinking with which I now confront the other person, the percept of him becomes, as it were, psychically transparent. As my thinking apprehends the percept, I am compelled to judge that what I perceive is really quite other than it appears to the outer senses. The sensuous appearance, it being what it immediately is, reveals something else which it is mediately. In presenting itself to me, it at the same time extinguishes itself as a mere sensuous appearance. But in thus extinguishing itself it reveals something which compels me as a thinking being to extinguish my own thinking as long as I am under its influence and to put its thinking in the place of mine. Its thinking is then apprehended by my thinking as an experience like my own. Thus I have really perceived another's thinking…It is a process which passes wholly in my consciousness and consists in this, that the other's thinking takes the place of my thinking. Through the self-extinction of the sensuous appearance the separation between the spheres of the two consciousnesses is actually abolished.[cci]

It is necessary to understand that Steiner does not see thinking as some kind of lamp that we shine onto reality, which shows reality to us, and which does not affect that reality in so shining, adds nothing to it. Rather, thinking is one half of the original whole.

Interpenetration

What is interpenetration? Sartre conceives it as a 'mixing together'—like cream with coffee—of the three temporal ekstases of the for-itself as an in-itself. These temporal 'parts' are connected irrationally, acting on one another as if by "sympathetic magic acting from a distance." This irrationality is inescapable, and denies "psychic forms" (including feelings) the status of the ontological. These forms are of merely psychological status; there is no connection of consciousness with consciousness, for-itself with for-itself.

Sartre argues that pure reflection—"the simple presence of the for-itself to the for-itself reflected on"—inevitably results in failure, insofar as it is an attempt again by the for-itself to be what it is, which, however it is tried, will always fail. This is because, for Sartre, consciousness is for, it is intentional. Steiner, on the other hand, argues that thinking, though intentional, when turned on itself, is still of the same kind as its object, and thus remains thinking through and through. Instead of focusing on being, Steiner considers the species of being, and finds that reflection on thinking involves no infinitely regressive analysis.

It is clear to me that what Sartre describes in "The Existence of Others" is in fact more consistent with Steiner's argument that what in fact is going on is the replacement of my thinking by the thinking of the Other. Insofar as that other thinking attends to the percepts marking that Other, namely, the percepts of my body, then my being-for-others is exactly that, my being as the Other experiences me. Steiner argues that this replacement goes unnoticed because thinking replaces thinking, thus there is no break in quality; and also because the oscillations from one to the other occur so rapidly.

Sartre's descriptions fit exactly with Steiner's account of what is going on when we are looked at by the Other: the look of the Other "hides his eyes; he seems to go in front of them...[T]he look is upon me without distance." We cannot mean the Other's body comes out in front, for it is that (which Steiner calls the "sensuous appearance") that is eclipsed. Sartre describes this as an illusion, but I see no reason that it should be; that "my perception [should] decompose and pass into the background" when I attend to the look is fundamental, and ought to be regarded as such. For Sartre, besides perception there is only being-in-itself and being-for-itself, thus we must have encountered one or the other in the look. Being-for-others is indistinguishable from the Other's being-for-me, and there is no reason to attribute it to a different relation from that which accounts for the former, namely, being-for-itself—thinking.

Perhaps one other point to make concerns a little closer look at what we mean by interpenetration. Sartre's facetious example is the cream in the coffee. But if we demand an atomistic analysis of our conceptions, then I doubt that we would consider even the cream in the coffee as true interpenetration, for at some level we would imagine that one could theoretically distinguish if not actually separate the different molecules and atoms from each other. Thus we have a mixture, and not interpenetration. Instead, if we are to understand interpenetration, it must be without parts, in an atomistic sense. Sartre's phenomenology of the Other is exactly that. "We are dealing with a relation which is without parts, given at one stroke."[ccii] To my mind, this is exactly the field in which interpenetration can be understood to obtain. Thus does Coleridge speak well to us in this matter:

> It is a dull and obtuse mind, that must divide in order
> to distinguish; but it is a still worse, that distinguishes in
> order to divide.[cciii]

This observation may be well considered regarding the environment.

Steiner's suggestion of the rapidity of the replacement, and the fact of the homogeneous quality of the replacement, seems simpler to me than Sartre's being-for-others. Besides, the 'collapse' of the for-itself into objectivity seems to contradict all that Sartre says about the for-itself. Sartre has described well the phenomena, but he does slip into hypothesis which is unnecessarily complex.

Detachment and Boundaries

The contemporary clinical notion of co-dependence assumes an interpenetration between subjects, between consciousnesses, and "recovery" is the process of detaching from harmful and debilitating enmeshment by establishing boundaries for oneself. The co-dependent self is "[a]lienated from the True Self…is other-oriented, i.e., focuses on what it thinks others want it to be; it is over-conforming."[cciv] Co-dependence "is a dependence on people and things outside the self, along with neglect of the self to the point of having little self-identity."[ccv] It is "an emotional, psychological, and behavioral pattern of coping that develops as a result of an individual's prolonged exposure to, and practice of, a set of oppressive rules—rules which prevent the open expression of feelings."[ccvi] It is "an unhealthy and abnormal disease

process...[which leads] to a process of nonliving which is progressive."[ccvii] It "makes life painful."[ccviii]

> We can begin to define co-dependence as any suffering
> and/or dysfunction that is associated with or results from
> focusing on the needs and behaviors of others. Co-
> dependents become so focused upon or preoccupied with
> important people in their lives that they neglect their True
> Self.[ccix]

The phenomenon of co-dependence grew out of the study and treatment of alcoholism, and characterized whoever was in a close relationship
with the alcoholic. Charles Whitfield diagrams the co-dependent family
this way:[ccx]

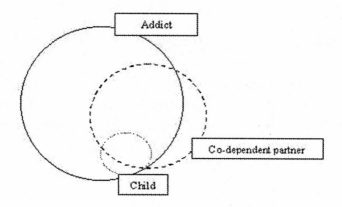

Where the largest circle represents the alcoholic or somehow
addicted individual, the smaller dotted circle represents the co-dependent partner or spouse, and the smallest circle represents the child. An
important feature of the co-dependent family is that it usually has a
secret. This is important to the dynamics of co-dependence, especially
insofar as the co-dependent family is "shame based," that is, where the

basis of communication between the members is shame, where shame is defined as feeling bad "from being something wrong or bad."ccxi Shame is thus distinguished from guilt, which is to feel bad for doing something wrong or bad. Secretiveness disables the members of the family

> because being secretive prevents the expression of questions, concern and feelings (such as fear, anger, shame and guilt). And the family thus cannot communicate freely."ccxii

Communication, verbal communication, is clearly the most important tool we have to state our purposes, needs, and limits, and to ask questions, clarify ambiguities, and challenge assumptions.

Thus it is perhaps to be seen that the implied treatment of co-dependence, in part, is to be a shift in thinking from the other's point of view to one's own point of view, so that the True Self is allowed expression by eliminating or reducing oppression. This "detachment," as it is often called, involves the recognizing and acknowledging of one's own needs, and one's own being, as a first step. It is detachment insofar as it is a withdrawal from the experience of the other's needs, a preoccupation which blinds the co-dependent to their own needs. Thus an intimate but healthy relationship looks like this:ccxiii

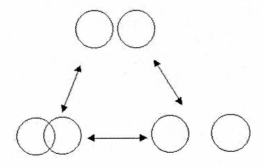

which depicts boundaries that are dynamic, and which have "a flexible ebb and flow that respects each member's needs and allows each to grow as individuals."ccxiv

I want to suggest that the literature of co-dependency, as well as the therapeutic treatment of it, specifically with regard to enmeshment and detachment, makes little sense if it is not so that we can and do apprehend the thinking of other's. If one understands the boundaries discussed above in terms of Steiner's analysis of encounters with the other, then the first diagram depicts a situation where the oscillation between one's own consciousness and its replacement by the consciousness of another is almost non-existent. Almost all the time, one's thinking is replaced by that of the other.

Such a supposition would be for Sartre a bad faith exercise, if I am positing "psychic forms" as the thinking, the consciousness, of another, with which I am enmeshed. But as I have already argued, the Other's "point of view" is yet a consciousness of, and thus a for-itself, for it is myself that is being nihilated. It is the Other's view of me which I as co-dependent maintain, to my detriment. Thus this is not merely psychological, and therefore derived from the ontological.ccxv Sartre is correct in arguing that an in-itself-for-itself—the objective of the attempt by the for-itself to be what it is—is impossible, and the interpenetration of mere psychic forms is the description of just such an in-itself-for-itself. But I am arguing from Steiner's view for a for-itself replaced by another for-itself, not an in-itself-for-itself.

Further, the fact that severe co-dependency is often experienced as a painful, mentally anguishing alienation and 'non-being,' as a denial of needs and lack of emotion that are "mine", suggests both the shifting nature of consciousness—it can reside outside of me—and its contingent homing nature—it hurts to have it always out there. This pain can in fact be viewed as the consequence of the denial of my being in shame. Co-dependence, then, can be seen in part as the inability to balance out the replacement of my thinking by that of the other by establishing a more permanent home for my own thinking. Whitfield's diagrams depict this nicely.

Thus does it seem to me that, in light of Steiner's account of the encounter of the Other, together with a brief consideration of the phenomenon and treatment of co-dependency, Sartre's phenomenological descriptions of the look of the Other are not best explained by his ontology, but by Steiner's interpenetration of consciousnesses. This interpenetration is assumed in co-dependence recovery, and aims toward an initial detachment and a subsequently more balanced oscillating movement between consciousnesses.

The Non-Human Other

I have found Sartre's phenomenology of the Other to be particularly helpful in seeing more clearly my own experiences of encounters with non-human nature.[ccxvi] Especially enlightening is Sartre's account of the crackling branches behind one as they walk along a path: "I apprehend immediately…not that there is someone there,"[ccxvii] but that I am here. This very experience I have had again and again as I have peered into the mountains from afar. All of a sudden, they extinguish themselves, dissolve, liquify, even as 'I,' my body, my self, rises up as it hardens. 'I' am looking from the mountain; 'I' am the mountain, seeing 'me' in the valley. I have looked up into valleys between mountain peaks, valleys that turn back behind the peaks and out of sight, only to have my own face touched by— myself. I find myself looking at me.

Steiner argues that it is thinking that posits 'subject' and 'object,' and thus cannot itself be merely subjective. He argues that concepts, though borne by an ego-consciousness, do not originate there, but are universal and common to all. Thus in bearing the concept "triangle," for instance, I grasp or bear the very same concept which anyone else does who thinks that concept. In this regard it is thinking itself which posits the concepts 'me' and 'mountain.' It is thinking that, though when permeating mathematically/perspectivally uniquely situated percepts marks out the region of reality, is not bound to those percepts, including percepts of self. Sartre's ontology does not prohibit such an 'upsurge' of consciousness. In fact, it supports it, in that the phenomenology of the look is more simply accounted for by Steiner as the actual apprehension of the thinking of another. It is thinking interpentrating thinking, self- and world-consciousness together in one place at one time.

Insofar as such interpenetration as Steiner describes is valued by anyone concerned to relate with wildness in a caring and conscientious way, then such recovery work as described in the previous section may prove very, very valuable. I have briefly described my own experiences with the mountains, and want to suggest that in fact what I have experienced there is the replacement of my consciousness with that of the mountains, or mountain. We are learning from many quarters that we are not merely boxes of bone and flesh inside of which we carry a kind of airy thinking substance. Rather we are more like interpenetrating complexes of relations. It is not so great a leap, then, to suppose that that field of interpenetration is replete with the voices, the thinking, of many, many others. Thus have I heard the thinking of a mountain; I have seen myself as the mountain has seen me. If this is so, this complicated field of thinking and perception, then what is called for is an increasingly lively dance of detachment and intimacy.

Environmentalists in particular may find this shamefully ignorant, on two counts. First, some deny any kind of human sentience or consciousness to nature, to wildness; some deny it categorically, others as an unjustifiable but not absolutely verifiable projection. But it seems to me that their own ecocentrism is either that same projection, or it must be some kind of quasi-homeless, i.e., transcendent consciousness. Second, some deny not consciousness but interpenetration: the wild is not me, and cannot be me. But this just seems another version of the 'ghost in the machine' view of being, including human being, which view they would deny is valid.

Besides, the co-dependency view suggests that what an interpenetrating world involves if it is going to work is not Sartre's alienation and rejection, but detachment and care. Coleridge's sentiment, as well, can be a very valuable guide, in that we are not about chopping up the world to see how it works; we are about learning how to live respectfully and carefully in the heart of being. That is the lesson and fact of interpenetration. The boundaries and cycles of interpenetration will have to be learned and practiced, and they will have to be learned and practiced from within. This is exactly what George Sessions suggests at the end of his essay, "Ecocentrism, Wilderness, and Global Ecosystem Protection":

> To experience the [shift from an economically exploitive world view and society to an ecological 'green' society] no doubt requires a conversion to an ecological consciousness, an 'ecological self,' or what Paul Taylor refers to as an 'inner change.'[ccxviii]

And what do we mean by 'inner' if not consciousness, and what do we mean by starting there, if we have already declared that consciousness is merely human and thus has no place in our talk of the wildness of nature?

Such a shift I think can be valuably regarded as a spiritual movement, if spirituality regards the inner life as important and real, and addresses it deliberately and with care; without a doubt, recovery from co-dependence involves a dimension of spirituality. "[S]pirituality is about the relationships that we have with our self, with others, and with the universe."[ccxix]

Spirituality is the last stage in our recovery. Paradoxically, it can never be a stage, since it is an ongoing process throughout suffering, healing and serenity.[ccxx]

Finally, if one sees language, both oral and written, as midway between the direct encounter with the human other, on the one hand, and with non-human nature, on the other, then Barfield's claim implicit in *Saving the Appearances* that one can, in the history of language, encounter the different qualities of consciousness that have preceded one's one, is satisfyingly intelligible.

Science, History, and Sensibility

Introduction

There are two key connections, or questions, that link the discussion of Barfield's evolution of consciousness with the history of philosophy:

1. Do ancient, medieval, early modern, and oriental texts express collections of differing opinions regarding a common and unchanging objective world, or do they express different thinking and therefore different worlds?

2. Do consciousnesses interpenetrate?

This chapter lays out a direct answer to the first question, in the domain of the history and philosophy of science. The implications of that answer constitute an answer to the second question.

Barfield was quite deliberate in his consideration of science—its history, its method, its practice, its logical underpinnings. The main reason for this consideration was his conviction that, distinct from the actual practice of science, there was the worldview that nurtured that practice. That worldview, which he most often meant when he used the word "science," was, *qua* worldview, held in common with and as the western world. He did not consider himself an enemy of the practice of science, in general, but rather he devoted himself to bringing to the surface the assumptions of the worldview, which were also the assumptions of the practice. Those assumptions as a complex is what he meant by the term "idolatry."

In the discussion that follows, we take a more direct look at the history and philosophy of science, and consider what some other thinkers have concluded regarding the assumptions of both the worldview and the practice of science. We will see that, implicit in the discussions of these other thinkers is the question regarding the interpenetration of consciousnesses. It is the question itself, as well as any answer to it, that constitutes the new radical nature of history.

I

Since Thomas Kuhn's *The Structure of Scientific Revolutions*[ccxxi] reshaped the history of science, history and science have been rather problematically related. Insofar as philosophy has been, for the last two hundred years or so, the apologist for and self-consciousness of science, these developments in the history of science have troubled philosophers as well.[ccxxii] What has been perhaps most troubling to philosophers, what has generated much discussion, is the notion of incommensurability. Kuhn himself puts it this way:

> What differentiated these various schools was not one
> or another failure of method…but what one shall come to
> call their incommensurable ways of seeing the world and
> of practicing science in it.[ccxxiii]

Kuhn speaks of "ways of seeing the world," as well as the perhaps more rational "practice" of science. In *Against Method,* Paul Feyerabend too regards perception as involved in the notion of incommensurability, and casts the history of science and the role of philosophy in the development of that history in an even more stark light. He suggests that studies in the development of perception in children show that in proceeding from infancy to adulthood, individuals proceed from perceptual experience incommensurable with what follows.

> Now is it reasonable to expect that conceptual and perceptual changes of this kind occur in childhood only?…Or is it more realistic to assume that fundamental changes, entailing incommensurability, are still possible…? Besides, the question of the mobility of the adult stage is at any rate an empirical question that must be attacked by research, and cannot be settled by methodological fiat. The attempt to break through the boundaries of a given conceptual system is an essential part of such research…[ccxxiv]

There are many other books in which this incommensurability is discussed, all with interesting results. Near the end of his book *Coming to Our Senses: Body and Spirit in the Hidden History of the West,*[ccxxv] Morris Berman summarizes his argument up to that point that

> Western history is profoundly discontinuous; that it crosses certain watersheds, or undergoes certain system-breaks, such that what is regarded as real or relevant on one side of the 'fault line' becomes inconsequential on the other…[ccxxvi]

Bruno Snell in his The Discovery of the Mind: The Greek Origins of European Thought[ccxxvii] considered the task of accessing the antecedent of "thought" as difficult but not impossible, suggesting that there is such a thing as "accessibly incommensurable" ways of being, and he went on to trace out those origins. Berman also discusses the inherent difficulties in describing an admitted "hidden history," but describes such a history, and optimistically discusses methodological concerns nonetheless.

In environmental philosophy, philosophers have often discussed incommensurability, often together with the notion of alternative conceptual schemes/frameworks.[ccxxviii] Phrases such as "different worlds" and "constructing reality" have become almost commonplace in some circles, especially that circle pejoratively labeled New Age. The breadth of the circulation of these notions of historical discontinuity and the related notion of different worlds is quite impressive. The previous chapter demonstrated at the least that this notion occupied mainstream philosophy for a time, and still does.

Finally, in anthropology and linguistics this notion of "different worlds" began its career quite early on in the writings of Edward Sapir and Benjamin Lee Whorf (the latter whom Feyerabend discusses briefly but importantly in *Against Method*). This is a very telling treatment of incommensurability, because anthropologists are presumably studying what in many other respects is, if not other worlds, as close to it as one can get.

Underlying "different worlds", then, is the notion of incommensurability. It is difficult to say why "incommensurability" emerged as a topic of concern for philosophers of science, but it can be stated with certainty when this happened. Thomas Kuhn was the first to use the word as a philosophically significant term, in *The Structure of Scientific Revolutions*. Kuhn's conclusion was that the difference between "competing schools" of science was essentially the "incommensurable ways of seeing the world" that characterized each. It is not accidental that early in Kuhn's historical studies he was directed to "the experiments by which Jean Piaget has illuminated both the various worlds of the growing child and the process of transition from one to the next."[ccxxix] Perception was early implicated in his thoughts regarding the development of science.

Judging from the indices of various books on the philosophy of science, "incommensurability" was not a topic of discussion until after Kuhn published *The Structure of Scientific Revolutions*. Related notions and concerns were being approached, though. R.G. Collingwood published *The Idea of History* in 1946; Bruno Snell's *The Discovery of the Mind* was published in 1953 in English; Benjamin Lee Whorf's *Language, Thought, and Reality* was published in 1956, but the essays therein date from as early as 1927, and the essay "Linguistics and Science" was published in 1940. He concludes there that

> [o]ne significant contribution to science from the linguistic point of view may be the greater development of our sense of perspective. One shall no longer be able to see a few recent dialects of the Indo-European family, and the rationalizing techniques from their patterns, as the apex of the evolution of the human mind, nor their present wide spread as due to any survival from fitness or to anything but a few events of history—events that could be called fortunate only from the parochial point of view of the favored parties. They, and our own thought processes with them, can no longer be seen as spanning the gamut of reason and knowledge but only as one constellation in a galactic expanse.[ccxxx]

Michael Polanyi published *Personal Knowledge* in 1958; and Barfield's own *History in English Words* in 1926 began his lifelong discussion of the evolution of consciousness.

As a philosophically interesting and significant term "incommensurability" began its career with Kuhn's *Scientific Revolutions*.

> What differentiated these various schools was not one or another failure of method—they were all "scientific"— but what we shall come to call their incommensurable ways of seeing the world and of practicing science in it.[ccxxxi]

This he says in his "Introduction: A Role for History." Right away Kuhn involves all of philosophy of science in the discussion: historicist concerns, realist concerns, logical and analytical concerns. Insofar as philosophy in America was at that time considered most importantly an analysis of science and the scientific worldview, then *all* of philosophy was involved.

Kuhn's book is an articulation of the statement quoted above, and all his later work is the pounding out of various details, and the answering of many objections, to the central thesis of "incommensurability." The chapters entitled "Revolutions as Changes of World View" and "The Invisibility of Revolutions" contain the most controversial material; this material has acquired the most extensive explication (or intensive refutation?) in philosophy. Themes therein include: the meaning of "world" and "paradigm," the nature and significance of *gestalt* switches and the role of psychological dimensions of human activity in philosophical discussions of science, theory-laden perception, neutral observation language, and cumulativity of scientific knowledge. Themes that have been spawned by Kuhn's work, and by the apparently corroborative writings of others, include translation questions, realism and relativism debates, alternative conceptual schemes, the standing of logical empiricism, historicity, theory and language, rationality, and the viability of philosophy itself.

One constellation of concerns that have not come up in philosophy in the course of discussing incommensurability are those of quality and qualities, morality, and human values in general. These matters have apparently been the concern of sociologists, philosophically minded scientists, historians, and generalists, like Theodore Roszak, Albert Einstein, Werner Heisenberg, Carl Sagan, David Bohm, Fritjof Capra, Heinz Pagels, and Morris Berman. Perhaps the only philosophers treating such concerns with any follow-through are the multitude of environmental philosophers, but they are for the most part ignored in the wider philosophical community, judging by references to them in more traditional journals and venues. All this begins to suggest the seminal and ovarial quality of Kuhn's incommensurability in *The Structure of Scientific Revolutions*, and the influence it has had on the character of philosophy in the latter half of the twentieth century.

The issues involved in coming to terms with Kuhn's book have been varied and numerous. In the mid-Seventies the references in philosophical work to Kuhn and his *Scientific Revolutions* blossomed. "Incommensurability" in particular finds a place of its own in *The Philosopher's Index* headings beginning in 1974, and has missed entries only one year since. In Frederick Suppe's *The Structure of Scientific Theories*[ccxxxii] Kuhn gets almost two pages of the index to himself; "incommensurability" is discussed on approximately thirty pages in all of the text. This was only seven years after *Scientific Revolutions* was published.

The discussions involving incommensurability are manifold, as Suppe describes in the introduction of *Scientific Theories*, but the aspects of concern are charges that Kuhn renders scientific "progress" an irrational process, that it commits us to epistemological relativism, and that meanings of terms change from one theory to another.[ccxxxiii] This was the situation in the late Sixties in the philosophy of science, and the symposium on the structure of scientific theories, the proceedings of which form the core of Suppe's book, was a kind of emergency meeting to discuss the collapse of that philosophical discipline.

Kuhn brought in history as an expert witness to testify that scientific practice and theory undergo changes on the order of revolutions. Pre- and post-revolution "paradigms" of scientific practice are so different as to make intelligible the claim that the practitioners in those different paradigms practice in different worlds. Granted that theories on opposite sides of the revolution are incommensurable with one another, that they cannot be compared in any straightforward and conclusive way, then theory choice becomes a matter of....Well, it is no longer a simple matter of logical analysis; it must involve other standards, but which look more like personal tastes than rational considerations.

At this many philosophers balked, accusing Kuhn of reducing science to irrational politicking and hobbyhorse riding. Apparently that charge in itself was assumed sufficient to justify rejection of the testimony of history; Kuhn's work represented the *reductio ad absurdum* discounting such a notion. Paul Feyerabend, in *Against Method*, suggests instead that such rejection only shows the irrational commitment to philosophers' dreams of objectivity and the hegemony of the scientific worldview, and no more. Judging by the response of the philosophical community to Feyerabend's work on this score, the validity of the testimony of *reductio ad absurdum* is regarded more highly (felt much deeper) than the facts of history.

Very closely associated with the rejection of the imputation of such irrationality to scientific progress was the rejection of the relativism implied by Kuhn's account. Kuhn argued that theoretical apparatus was part and parcel of an entire paradigm of scientific practice, including and especially all the textbook training that an aspiring scientist acquired. This "disciplinary matrix" as he later called it was the "world" in which the particular theory was to be understood; the theory was relative to that matrix, and the world was relative to the theory. Nature itself fluxed with human minds, and the prospect of the disappearance of any firm footing for our knowledge of the world seemed again too much to believe for many philosophers.

The issue of meaning change, as closely tied in with the previous two concerns as those two with one another, is at least more specific and perhaps tangible than the former issues, and seemingly more easily refuted. What could be easier than to show that the meaning of a word has or has not changed? Instead, that issue was at least near the center of concern, and apparently of debate, in the 1969 symposium: What is the meaning of scientific theories? What is the meaning of theoretical terms? Questions like these were at both fore- and background at that conference, and in the wider philosophical literature of the time. Both on a micro and macro level, meaning was slipping through the analytical fingers of the philosophy of science.

In his Afterword of 1977, Suppe called attention, then, to the swan song of positivism, and traced the first baby steps of philosophy of science on the road toward a "Metaphysical and Epistemological Realism." He urged the reader to see the resolution, imperfect as it may be, of the profound disarray witnessed in the late Sixties and early Seventies within philosophy of science, accompanied (evidenced?) by "The Waning of the Weltanschauungen Views," the most notable of the latter being Kuhn's history of scientific revolutions and incommensurable disciplinary matrices.

What has come since Suppe's Afterword seems in part to attest to his observations: the debate between relativism and realism is a healthy and involved one at present, and has been for at least five years.[ccxxxiv] At the same time, incommensurability will not go away, and continues to get dragged into plenty of discussions in the philosophy of science today. In particular, philosophers ask where incommensurability can be said to obtain: between theories, between experimental methodologies, between percepts as witnessed by different scientists, or somewhere else? Others are asking *how* incommensurability might obtain. Still others are digging deep to understand the psychology of *gestalt* switches: given the experimental results in perceptual psychology that cannot be ignored, must one concur with those who insist that theoretical commitments influence perception (is all perception theory-laden?) and therefore the implication of different worlds for different theories?

II

Kuhn claimed that scientists working according to differing paradigms work in different worlds. He argued that revolutionary changes in method and theory were precipitated by accumulation of anomalous experimental data, which 'forced' the adoption of a new paradigm, by way of abandonment of the old. He discussed findings in *Gestalt* psychology to illustrate what he took to be somehow central to the crisis of paradigm change, and that is perception. Revolutionary 'seeing' is a kind of seeing for the first time,' a

> relatively sudden and unstructured event like the *gestalt* switch. Scientists then often speak of the 'scales falling from the eyes' or of the 'lightning flash' that 'inundates' a previously obscure puzzle...[ccxxxv]

That work in psychology and perception "makes one suspect that something like a paradigm is prerequisite to perception itself. [Otherwise] there can only be, in William James' phrase, 'a bloomin' buzzin' confusion.'"[ccxxxvi]

Are these claims so radical? The reaction in philosophy was quite strong and involved, at least in terms of numbers of articles written—eventually—and the number of issues seen to be related. One might argue that in some sense his claims about the role of paradigms in perception itself are only neo-Kantian variations. If that is so, why the strong reaction?

That there is more involved can be seen in the work of Paul Feyerabend. One of the more general but telling criticisms of Kuhn's work is that, after all has been said and done, and he has responded to his critics by modifying his claims, he ends up with a position that is not as vulnerable to criticism, maybe, but also is not nearly so philosophically interesting. The seeds of Kuhn's moderation are seen in the original work. In the chapter "Revolutions as Changes of World View" he describes a paradigm shift "as if...." But then he ends his musings this way:

> Of course, nothing of quite that sort does occur: there
> is no geographical transplantation; outside the laboratory
> everyday affairs usually continue as before.[ccxxxvii]

Further on he states that whatever changes do occur as aspects of a paradigm shift, they are "never total. Whatever he may then see, the scientist after a revolution is still looking at the same world."[ccxxxviii]

Feyerabend takes Kuhn's work to its more radical and consistent conclusions. Though he is no disciple of Kuhn, and has often been his critic, Feyerabend is concerned with the notion of incommensurability in the history and philosophy of science, and that notion is the heart of Kuhn's book. The radical character of the notion is evident in Feyerabend more than in Kuhn, partly because Kuhn seems intent on making the notion as uncontroversial as possible, but also because Feyerabend seems intent on making of it the scandal of philosophy of science. Frederick Suppe argues that Kuhn has lost what was attractive (or repulsive, but still philosophically interesting) in the notion by moderating his views, while Feyerabend has lost all credibility because he will not listen to his critics (he will not modify his views).[ccxxxix]

Much of the burden of the contemporary critique of science, especially with regard to objections to exclusive claims to knowledge, has been borne by new histories of science and of thought in general. Critics and reformers like Feyerabend and Kuhn have done much to show that systems and practices previous to the modern scientific ones are not commensurable with those modern ones. History is very important to a proper understanding of science today, but this is true especially because history is itself being understood in a new way.

Re-reading the history texts, especially historical introductions to science texts, will do no good beyond reminding one of what they are up against as far as the modern picture of the past is concerned. Feyerabend thinks so, and the new paradigm of historical research toward which Feyerabend moves is this chapter's main topic. The relation between that new paradigm and the passing of the old science is another.

The work of both Kuhn and Feyerabend, including specifically the notion of incommensurability, has undergone plenty of scrutiny over the last twenty to thirty years, by philosophers, sociologists, psychologists, and others. It is not surprising that this notion has not met with unqualified approval, nor comprehension either. One of the criticisms of this notion of theirs is that it is unintelligible and unhelpful as a tool of understanding the history of science.

The method that Feyerabend is against is that which most historians and philosophers of science ascribe to science: the all-logical, super-powerful, ever-consistent inductive method. Feyerabend rejects the view of science that reveals a steady development of knowledge that has been made possible and is guided by a method that prescribes logical consistency within a given theory, and rational, defensible, empirically substantiated transitions from one theory to another, transitions which always result in an increase in knowledge ("empirical content"), entailing a subsumption of preceding theory by later theory.

Feyerabend argues that the orthodox rationalist story of science does not fit the facts: Galileo, hero of rationalism, used propaganda, persuasion, and sophisticated but nonetheless circular reasoning to defend Copernicanism. He substantiated new facts with other new, unsubstantiated facts or theories. He invented new natural interpretations. Feyerabend further argues that the orthodox story describes a method that in fact stops all progress of science.

In arguing this second point, he looks at both orthodox method (that is, method as the philosophers see it), and historical practice to show that no such orthodox method could ever work to bring about what one actually sees today as science; such a method would only preserve the status quo. Opposed to the orthodoxy of method Feyerabend discovers counter-induction, or 'anything goes.'[ccxl] Feyerabend argues from history and conceptually that it is in fact counter-induction rather than induction that best describes the character and development of science as history shows it. Counter-induction is just what it sounds like: proceeding on non- or ir-rational grounds in order to develop a new thesis or to substantiate a new claim. This entails a fundamental incommensurability of different scientific theories, as opposed to a rational, dialectic, smooth development of scientific knowledge over time. Incommensurability here is the claim that differing world views are really as the term suggests, views of different worlds, rather than merely differing points of view of the same world, and that those worlds cannot be brought together merely by a rational method of equating term to term.

Feyerabend speaks of this incommensurability in terms of a heterogeneity of knowledge, the qualitatively varied texture of knowledge. When one considers theories one not only deals with concepts rationally and logically connected and corresponding to empirical observation, but also with tradition that is fundamentally somatic. These polar opposites, and everything in between, have varied through history: today "gravity" is more nearly conceptual than somatic, and weight more nearly somatic than conceptual, whereas for Isaac Newton, gravity was more somatic than conceptual.

In the face of a "world of science [that] has the power to push aside alternatives and the entities they postulate"[ccxxli] Feyerabend says, "everything goes!" He calls for an epistemological and methodological anarchism, demands separation of science and state which coalition only serves to maintain the status quo, and applauds creationists' attempts to get creationism taught alongside evolution in schools. He wants to dethrone Reason, for the sake of continuing to make history.

How does one continue to make history? One counter-induces; one avails oneself to whatever works; one adopts a pragmatic philosophy of participation, as opposed to an attitude of mere observation. Tradition is partly responsible for the status and change of science, tradition not only in the sense of stories being passed on in culture, especially via textbooks today, but also as somatic practice. Kuhn's paradigm shift was not merely a logical or dialectical process, but a discontinuous one; it was a crisis brought on by the accumulation of anomalous data. In response to criticisms that "paradigm" "confused two quite distinct notions,"[ccxlii] Kuhn instead spoke of a "disciplinary matrix,"[ccxliii] which has many of the characteristics of the earlier "paradigm." Included in both notions is that of *actual laboratory practice*: instrumentation and experimentation. Actual somatic practices that involve manipulation and configuration of, and participation in, apparatus, change from, and *mark,* one era to the next. As such, they are "not amenable to a fully explicit characterization."[ccxliv]

Incommensurability describes the relation between different somatic disciplines, in part. Kuhn focuses on the practices of scientists as scientists, but surely the term "disciplinary matrix" allows of a quite broad description. On this account Kuhn's successor to "paradigm" has fared little better than its predecessor. For present purposes, the breadth of the valid application of the description does not render it ineffectual, but rather points up the importance of all somatic practice in the formation of one's worldview as a "disciplinary matrix."

One's discipline begins in earnest at least at birth. By the time that one is an adult, one can look over one's entire lifetime, and begin to perceive the actual shape of one's disciplinary matrix in those disciplined behaviors that span significant portions of one's life. Rather than a piecemeal or cross-section view, one has a broader but nonetheless detailed view of that matrix as such. Rather than speaking of a scientific matrix as not only distinct but discrete, one must speak of it as imbedded in the larger pattern; and vice versa.[ccxlv] It is from this view that Feyerabend speaks of tradition as something "only rarely in our control."[ccxlvi] This tradition undermined all the theories leading up to the present.

A radical, and to some a disturbing, implication of incommensurability is that atoms and gods are equally reasonable, neither having rational supremacy, defensible on rational grounds. It is history that has undermined the gods, in favor of atoms; rational discourse alone did not do it. One may then ask, "If history, not argument, undermined the gods, then what history are we talking about?"

In *The Discovery of the Mind* Snell traced out "the intellectual evolution of the Greek world."ccxlvii Snell in his introduction says that what he is after, the 'intellect' of the Greeks, "simply cannot be grasped in our speech."ccxlviii Anticipating a skeptical objection to his entire project, he continues:

Perhaps one shall be able to establish contact with Greek thought, not only through the medium of historical recollection, but also because the ancient legacy is stored in us, and one may recognize in it the threads of our own involved patterns of thinking.ccxlix

In Snell's analysis of the language of Homer and later Greeks, he saw a realignment of elements in the language on a syntactic level. For instance, in Homer there are many words for seeing, all of which have as their referents not aspects of the experience of vision, but rather what a seer looks like, how the eyes and face appear from the outside. In later Greek texts there are fewer words used to express seeing, and they soon are used in ways more like the present way to express more subjective aspects of seeing. This constriction of awareness, and the move from outer to inner experience, parallels Barfield's argument that meaning has constricted as a consequence of the constriction of perception. This is alpha-thinking, which focuses on the phenomena for their own sake. It also appears to be a somatic practice of literally focusing the eyes.

In his discussion of incommensurability Feyerabend refers to Snell's work to describe an incommensurable worldview, that of the ancient Greeks. He also adopts Benjamin Whorf's "covert classifications" as the cause of incommensurability, that is, that there are connections among concepts in a language "which operate...through an invisible 'central exchange' of linkage bonds in such a way as to determine other words which mark the class," and this invisible operation creates "patterned resistances to widely divergent points of view."[ccl] These resistances are not only the rejection of an alternative world view, but also the denial that what was presented was a different world view; one only sees a different point of view, or a different interpretation, of the same world.[ccli] These patterns of resistances are the "traditions" of a few paragraphs back that "are rarely in our control." Feyerabend adds to this a second thesis concerning incommensurability, "that the development of perception and thought in the individual also passes through stages which are mutually incommensurable."[cclii]

The preceding constitutes the beginnings of a description of incommensurability in terms that include "covert classifications," "invisible 'central exchange'," and somatic practice, with suggestions of mental or contemplative and bodily access and recovery of such a hidden history. Feyerabend is concerned with incommensurability (as a fact opposed to inductive homogeneity of knowledge and history of knowledge), Snell with the evolution of the intellect.

What if one takes both seriously?

Like Barfield, Snell and Feyerabend point to this development as the mark of an increase (the birth of!) self-consciousness. The importance of this development is that it shows not only a realignment of terms, but a constriction of terms, and thus also a correlative increase in self-consciousness. There are fewer words in Greek as time goes on that suggest a lack of focus on the percipient. The observer is increasingly implicated in the language itself.

Feyerabend argues further that, not only is there this development, but that it constitutes a move from one world to another which is incommensurable with what came before. Cosmology A must make room for a subsequent Cosmology B by slowly disappearing. This incommensurability is, then, largely a cognitive fact, in that cognition alone cannot span the gulf between that world and this. But this is not a denial of the possibility of knowledge of the preceding era. Barfield's work makes clear, and Feyerabend's hints at, the fact that a deliberate and self-conscious exercise of the imagination is the instrument of knowledge currently needed if the appearances are to be saved, if the gulf is to be spanned. In light of the preceding chapter's discussion of a Kantian phenomenal manifold, Barfield's final participation looks much more like the bodily practices that characterize incommensurable eras of consciousness. This imaginal thinking is not primarily discursive, and thus not hindered impossibly by somatic barriers. Not just language, but perception[ccliii] itself, the workings of the lens and pupil of the eye, has become increasingly constricted since the time of Homer.

Feyerabend says that tradition resists one's thinking; this is partly due to the fact that one denies the covert classifications, one denies the role that the bodily, somatic configuration plays in perception. He further says that though these traditions resist in places, they "are not the end and foundation of reasonable discourse."[ccliv] This suggests that traditions can change; and since they can change, and there is no rational way possible to decide which tradition is better, one must consider questioning the rationalist objective and resist the absolutizing of any one tradition.

The work of Feyerabend echoes Barfield's characterization of the evolution of consciousness as not merely a statement of significant difference between one age and another, but as a developmental difference that involves a loss. In this case, what has been lost is perceptual breadth and depth. Perception has become progressively constricted relative to pre-modern (and pre-adult) perception. At the same time, if there be authentic progression, or evolution, and not mere substitution, then something or other must remain constant through the loss. The implication here is that the scientific, constricted perception which one calls "objectivity," but which is also what one means by "common sense," was latent in that pre-modern perceptual world. What has been lost is the participation that characterized that perception.

This is the sense one must make of talk of incommensurability, and further, of access of tradition. To regard the present perceptual capacities as wanting (and not merely different) in some way relative to one's individual and racial past, is to allow for both a present growth, as well as an important past and ended growth. One's teeth come in, and then they fall out, making way not for an identical but new set, but a different and new set. Evolution, both individual and species, need be understood as something other than mere substitution. One can understand tradition in part as the somatic traces or analogs of what went before, such as a growth node on a tree branch, or the adult set of teeth. One then says with Feyerabend, "Never ever let any one tradition dominate!" in a developmental sense. Or, "Access your own tradition!" Or, "Access tradition for yourself!" The former refers to the individual vestiges stored somehow in the history and body of the individual; the latter refers to those racial or "special" (having to do with the species) vestiges accessible to the individual, beyond individual experience.

What has all this got to do with science? The prevailing world view is a scientific one, which is a constricted one, and it marks the latest contraction/constriction of consciousness, and not only the latest but the most qualitatively profound. This constriction marks the birth of self-consciousness on a large scale. This constriction has pushed humanity from the womb of compulsive participation, into the world of observation. Now one has the task of individually, self-consciously and willingly re-establishing for oneself that original participatory unity.

Does one want to do that, to reestablish such a unity, even if there were such a thing? Whether or no, many in fact feel the pain, and see the correlative phenomena of the present condition, phenomena which are atomic and unparticipated to a degree that can well be described as desperate. Snell and Feyerabend both suggest that there was no unity for the Greeks that was somehow behind the appearances. Barfield suggested in *Saving the Appearances* that this is because the appearances themselves were whole, were complete, were participated, and much broader than the present phenomena of Western culture.

The development of fewer and fewer words meaning "to see" is reflective not of a movement of unification, for what was happening was a constriction of perception, of awareness, of experience, which we recognize as Barfield's alpha-thinking. The extra-sensory elements of that experience lose their immediacy, and later show up as subjective and less certain qualities of reality. On this view, what the Greeks experienced as gods, and blades of sunlight penetrating the eyes, Plato saw as ideas, as forms, and the medievals conceived as universals, Galileo relegated to the status of secondary qualities, logical positivists labeled "subjective," and most today would totally or effectively deny any existence whatsoever. This is the world of science. Consciousness has contracted from the Homeric unselfconscious 'fitting into the pattern,' wherein all is conscious or aware, to the experience of today: a tiny spark of purely mental activity literally inside material brains, brains which are made of the very same stuff that all the rest of reality is.

If this constriction means confinement, there is hope yet that this tiny spark may yet light a way for a next step, not over into an intellectual anarchy, but down into the suppressed cosmology, the hidden history of one's own self, that must and will open up into the world of Homer, and even further back. This time, in Homer's world, "I" will be there.

III

If history shows a succession of incommensurable eras of thought and sensory experience, and if individuals also experience, in their individual histories, sequences of incommensurable eras, then it appears that the way of counter-induction is inward, at the tradition of the individual, by the individual. This imperative may be equal in importance to any scientific society-wide practice of counter-induction, and this is the sort of practice that Barfield meant to be the work of imagination, and called it final participation.

The task, whether seen as the overthrow of science or its reform, somehow involves practicing history, and a new kind of history at that. Assuming the present existential impasse and the scientific character of the age, this will involve a struggle to regain an awareness that has been lost, and that that effort will not involve regression, but rather expansion. In some way one does not return to the same place at all, but rather the analog of that previous experience in this new realm.

What does one actually do, what does the practice of this history look like? The field of this inquiry is what one now calls the un- or subconscious. Barfield had stated that the evolution of consciousness is also the history of the relationship between consciousness and unconsciousness. In *The Reenchantment of the World* Morris Berman makes a *prima facie* case for the identity between the body and the subconscious, via characteristics of a broad and reasonable contemporary notion of the subconscious.[cclv] In that case, the body and the breath suggest a natural starting point for the practice of a subterranean history.

Some, including some scientists,[cclvi] claim that whatever "practicing subterranean history" might be, it is to opt out of the present painful existence by merely withdrawing from it. Is it? Or is it a way to reestablish in a new way the only kind of unity that is appropriate to beings as self-conscious as humans are? Is this new history really a front for boldfaced cowardice or irresponsible and dangerous psychological self-experimentation, or the very work of new birth? There can be little doubt this is serious business, whether (serious) escapist fantasy, or the responsibility of every thoughtful and sincere person. Barfield admitted thatt a new way of history is not inherently or necessarily good; the sustained production of nonsense will become only too real if final participation is the case. But neither difficulty nor ease decide the question of whether this historical method is valid, only whether it will be desirable or possible.

Another question concerns the nature of the products of such a practice, the fruit, especially as contrasted with the overwhelming and undeniable success of the scientific mode of taking up with the world.

One may joke that the contemplative-as-clairvoyant can see into the distant past with incredible acuity, but cannot see anything through the wall into the next room, or into the mind of the person in the seat next to them. Assumptions of an empirical/materialistic sort go very deeply in such joking. If perception and conception have become constricted, then either empiricism must be abandoned, or our senses must be broadened, redeemed. If the latter notion is allowed even for a moment, it will seem quite reasonable that what one will be investigating in subterranean history will not be reducible to an empirical/material field: subconscious or subterranean phenomena will not exactly and only correspond 1:1 to the empirical/material phenomena.[cclvii] Because she cannot see into the next room with her microscope, and only into the leaf's cells, one does not laugh at the botanist. She has legs to get her into the next room, and then she can use her eyes.

Why bother with a subterranean history anyway? Many are experiencing an existential crisis. Yet it seems that behind this last question is the implicit answer, "Things aren't so bad." This depends mightily on what one means by "bad." Such a project of history may well be a responsibility to do what one can to sustain life on this planet, not just existence, but life, spiritual, moral, aesthetic. One wonders aloud, "We all feel it, and have at one time or another heard the life-negating claims of science, but when one goes to uncover the perpetrators, one only finds nice men and women in lab coats quietly and thoughtfully at work in their labs, whose looks of baffled hurt move us to shame for our cynicism and irresponsibility." Where then are those voices coming from? Why are so many eager to pin the blame on science? Why can no one make the charge stick? Maybe the voices are from within somehow. Maybe one needs to dream. Maybe one needs to remember that one dreamed once one wakes up. Maybe then the voices will either disappear, or one will soon know to whom they belong. At the least one will have become aware of yet another aspect of the real. That is what science is all about.

Short Studies in the Evolution of Consciousness

A philosopher once said that when one reads a text and comes across a term, a phrase, or a sentence that makes no sense, and is not further explained, then the reader ought to attempt to make sense of the text as a whole in light of that puzzling passage, rather than making sense of the puzzling passage in light of the rest of the text. From Barfield, the reader can add to this the clue of the "felt change of consciousness" that results from an encounter with such puzzles of meaning and interpretation. Barfield's own statements also affirm the wisdom of the approach suggested in the first sentence above. He said:

> Since participation is a *way* of experiencing the world in immediacy, and not a system of ideas about experience, or about the world, we obviously shall not find any contemporary *description* of it.... Our evidence [for participation] must be sought more often in what is implied or assumed than in what is actually affirmed. We can only reconstruct the collective representations of another age obliquely.[cclviii]

Finally, the reader should recall Barfield's explanation of the felt change of consciousness: the reader is participating in the consciousness that authored the text. With these tools, one is in a position to fairly test such a method of reading historical texts.

What is presented in this chapter are three, admittedly short studies that identify an opaque passage or obscure motivation, and ask the question, "Why?" "Why, in his *Meditations on the First Philosophy* did René Descartes seem to confuse abstractions with sensible objects?" "Why did John Locke begin *An Essay Concerning Human Understanding* by claiming to discredit the notion of innate ideas?" "Why did David Hume so vehemently argue that all ideas had their origin in sense impressions, but never even thought to address the sensible origin of the idea of resemblance?" The Barfieldian question that augments each of these is "What quality of consciousness would render these textual anomalies intelligible?" This is a different task than granting the current and prevailing worldview and then recasting the troublesome passages, terms, or motivations into the current vocabulary. By trying Barfield's approach, one may at least see whether or not such a way of reading leads to absurdity, or renders intelligible not only what was initially unintelligible at the start of the study, but also opens up other passages, and whole texts, to scrutability.

Descartes

In *Meditations on First Philosophy*, René Descartes demonstrated what he took to be the process of systematically considering the dubitability of all knowledge. He considered each sort of knowledge as he understood knowledge, and considered whether he could trust it or not. He reasoned that though waking cannot be indubitably distinguished from dreaming, nonetheless the elements of sense that constitute waking and dreaming are themselves indubitable. At least, the basic elements of waking and dreaming, namely, figure, extension, magnitude, place, and time. And at the very, very least—he proposed for the sake of his argument—whether in waking or dreaming, there is no doubting that 2+3=5.

In paragraph three of the First Meditation Descartes stated:

Everything which I have thus far accepted as entirely true and assured has been acquired from the senses or by means of the senses.

In paragraphs seven and eight he argued that, if waking may be dreaming, and dreaming be full of falsity as far as the images are concerned, still those images are made up of elements that are recognized as real in waking. This much is certain, he argued, namely, that corporeal nature in general and its extension, including shape, size, number, etc., are real.

These simple and universal concepts are true and existent, he continued, and corporeal nature and its extension are simple and universal entities, and are thus true and existent. But he then said immediately after that the sciences which concern themselves with these true and existent entities are not concerned with whether or not they occur in nature. The modern ear and mind are likely to hear and understand Descartes as saying that the sciences that are concerned with true and existent entities do not bother themselves with whether or not those entities exist!

A question regarding Descartes' reasoning so far is, Why does he end up talking about abstractions like figure, extension, and mathematical equations where he started out questioning the testimony of his senses? Arguably, Descartes' terminology in the *Meditations* is confusing. 'Concepts', 'elements', and 'entities' all refer to the same things. The modern reader makes a sharp distinction, though, between concepts and entities. At the beginning of this meditation, the reader assumes it is entities, that is, material and bodily and phenomenal experience that Descartes spoke of, as of course "sensory experience" of paragraph 3 suggested. But concepts are not phenomenal, and neither is the proposition $2+3=5$, nor is the truth of that proposition. Thus, though Descartes located the source of his doubtful opinions in his senses, everywhere in Descartes' work pertinent to the First Meditation it seems clear that perception was not the only source of Descartes' opinions. For why else would Descartes have discussed mathematics and geometry and arithmetic in a proof for the dubitability of opinions acquired from the senses?

Such a puzzle is usually answered simply that Descartes was a realist. He took numbers, mathematical entities, and elements (not objects) of perception to be real, in fact, more real than dubitable sensory experience. Given the history of the use of the category "realism," the puzzle is invisible to most readers; there is no puzzle. Descartes was a realist, that is how realists think. For the modern reader, the only real task is to follow Descartes' reasoning, and evaluate it on the basis of logical rules and known facts regarding the nature of reality. But given that Descartes eventually invoked God and characteristics of God as premises in his argument, the *material* validity of his argument is a foregone conclusion: it is invalid. The modern reader is left only with the bare logical structure of Descartes' arguments.

But the reader could engage this philosophical text quite differently. One could ask, "What would Descartes be assuming about the world that would make his confusion of abstractions and perceptions intelligible? What kind of world would make sense of Descartes' First Meditation?' To begin this train of questioning, the facts of the text would have to be reiterated, in order that the investigation remain true to them, rather than true to the very thing in question, namely, some system of the nature of reality. The most important fact to remember regarding this text, and the subject of the question above, is that Descartes undoubtedly confused notions that today are much more sharply distinguished: mathematical concepts and perceptual abstractions on the one hand, and perceptual experience on the other. In order to make this fact more clear, and thus to give credible direction to any conclusions, a contemporary and similar case to Descartes' apparent confusion (what might be regarded as a category mistake as Gilbert Ryle meant the term) will be considered.

Benjamin Whorf wrote a letter,[cclix] addressed to a Dr. English, the author of a dictionary of psychological terms, because, as Whorf put it to Dr. English,

> I have not been able to find in [your dictionary] or in any other source a recognized term for one of the phenomena in which I am interested and would like to know if you know of such a term or could suggest one.[cclx]

Imagine that one writes a professor of botany, asking her for the name of a plant that one came upon on one's walk up the mountainside. One tells her that the leaves had such and such a shape, and so many to a stem, and in a certain arrangement. One also tells her the colors, and the size, and even the character of the immediate environment. She would most likely be able to tell one quite accurately what it was that one saw. And given that she could do so, one would expect that she could even go further and state its scientific name, details of its growth cycle, its possible medicinal uses, if any, and many other useful and interesting facts concerning that plant. In fact, such additional information one would half expect, and such expectation would have motivated the correspondence in the first place.

In his correspondence to Dr. English, Whorf's "phenomena" is a kind of connecting of ideas that (apparently) has a definite character. This is evident by the fact that the "recognized term" in psychology for the connection of ideas—"association"—"will not do" for the meaning Whorf "has in mind."[cclxi] The definite character of the phenomena is further evident in the definite descriptions of experiments conducted to demonstrate the phenomena.[cclxii] Finally, Whorf speaks in definite negative terms (though only approximate positive terms) about the idea he has as it is in his mind:

I might say that my mental image of the relation is not at all one of ideas hitched together by bonds of attachment which they possess like miniature hooks and eyes. It is more a concept of continuity, with the ideas as relative locations in a continuous medium.[cclxiii]

Perhaps this is not at all neither unusual nor interesting. One speaks in definite terms of ideas all the time, or certainly could if the need or desire to do so ever arose. For instance:

> "What do you mean, exactly?"
> "Well, you know when you are in class and the teacher begins to discuss the reproductive system of humans, and all of a sudden you are aware of the girls in the class, and your face and ears begin to feel as if they are burning, and the more you try to control the burning the more you feel the burning, and you feel an urge to just hide somewhere? That is what I mean by 'embarrassment.'"

Yet, that is not the same kind of description as the above plant and botanist example, because there we had the phenomena, but no label. We had a definition, but no term. In the embarrassment example, we have the term *and* the phenomena. Whorf's case is like the plant and botanist example, since he had the phenomena at hand—in mind—but no term for it.

In Whorf's case, contrary to the other two, the term that is missing seems nearly indistinguishable, or inseparable, from the phenomena. The plant could have any name; what difference would it make to the description of it what it was called? The same with embarrassment: what difference would it make if it were called burning instead? Whereas in Whorf's case, the term itself was very important, at least to him, because so far as he knew, no one had named the phenomena to which he referred. The object here is the mind, or the stuff of the mind—ideas of mind. Though Whorf was discussing an idea, it is clear that it had some kind of substance for him, and could be investigated, and explicated, in a precise manner. It could be found.

It was just argued that embarrassment was like the plant, kinnikin-nik, for argument's sake, and that both were different from Whorf's term. Embarrassment is more like Whorf's term than kinnikinnik, and further, the differences are of an historical or chronological nature more than a semantic or empirical nature. That is, what can be seen in Whorf's musings, his mental, psychical exertion, is what once took place when embarrassment was coined, and when, even longer ago, kin-nikinnik was coined, and what might have taken place in Descartes' meditating.

Perhaps in the case of embarrassment the assertion is no more spectac-ular than in Whorf's case. The case of kinnikinnik is different. In that case the implication is that, at one time, kinnikinnik was no more (and no less) tangible for the one—or many—that coined the term to describe it than was Whorf's "a certain connection between ideas" for him, or corporeal entities were for Descartes. Consequently, Whorf's a-certain-connection-between-ideas could be, one day, as tangible as kinnikinnik, and material bodies, are now. Perhaps kinnikinnik was once like an idea is now.

It is clear that Whorf was not about some abstract mental exercise, some eviscerated mental calculation. He was not talking nonsense, nor in metaphors. If in fact Whorf's case is a look at what went on when embarass-ment, and even kinnikkinnik, were just beginning to become words, then in the evolution of such ideas one sees the very intimate relation that obtains between a term—a word—and its referent at such an early stage of its evolu-tion. In Whorf's case, the name he gave to the phenomena was as important to him, was as telling, as the phenomena itself. The term and the phenomena were consubstantial. The important difference between Whorf and Descartes, with regard to Barfield's epistemology of final participation, is that

Whorf's engagement with the psychically real was conscious and deliberate, and Descartes' was not.

Locke

The question, 'Why did Locke write this essay?' is an important one, for it relates to another question regarding his *Essay,* and that is, 'Why did Locke start out by discrediting the notion of innate ideas?' Why did he think it the necessary starting point for his essay?

In 1.IV.25, Locke referred to the notion of innate principles as the foundation and strength of the church/scholastic tradition before him. He determined that the tradition was founded on this, and that the tradition opposed or was contrasted to new developments in thought on this very point: whether or not humans could think independently or not. That independence had been proclaimed previously, but it was still not commonly understood. From the standpoint of that recognition, Locke attempted to show that there could not be innate principles, for that doctrine implied a certain moral as well as intellectual dependence or slavery, because innate principles, if there were such things, were inescapable, unavoidable, and undeniable. If they were the foundations of all knowledge, then all of knowledge was that way. Thus is the way to understand his arguments against the role of maxims in mathematics as the foundations of the truths in that science.

Locke was not attempting to do away with this doctrine with a mere few pages of argumentation. Rather, he was attempting to effect, affirm, and reinforce a break that had already begun. He was strengthening a position already assumed, to make it safer and more sure, and in this safety to investigate what he saw as the chief acquisition of that independence: the human understanding.

What he had to do was to construct a story about that rescued child that extricated the lad from any association with his previous circumstances that would thus implicate further slavery to those circumstances. Locke saw the human understanding as independent, in a way it had only recently been experienced, and he had to make sense of it without referring to that doctrine which denied it independence—the doctrine of innate principles. From that beginning he had to answer questions like, How then do we acquire knowledge? How can we be sure? What then is faith? And revelation? Belief? His answer was the essay itself.

To the question, Why did Locke start out by discrediting the notion of innate ideas? the answer appears to be, Locke did not begin by discrediting the notion of innate ideas, but by affirming the existence of such a thing as the human understanding, a something that could in fact, yet only very recently, be scrutinized. In order to make credible and intelligible that project of inquiring into the nature of the human understanding, he had to convince the reader that there was in fact such a thing.

Hume

Why did resemblance not perish, as causation did, as a metaphysical entity at the hand, by the pen and knife, of David Hume in *Treatise of Human Nature*? How come that relation forced itself gently yet irresistibly into Hume's mind, while causation faltered, betrayed its weakness, submitted to Hume's razor sharp dialectic? How were causation and resemblance different? How were they the same? How did they resemble? What was at the back of the sword stroke that severed Hume from the outside world? What was at the back of the habit of mind that constituted the human understanding, that grounded and quickened it? What was at the back of Hume's empiricism, and at the heart of his skepticism?

There are four words in Latin that convey something of the qualities of resemblance, and the histories of those qualities:

Convenientia:

> Those things are 'convenient' which come sufficiently close to one another to be in juxtaposition; their edges touch, their fringes intermingle, the extremity of the one also denotes the beginning of the other. In this way,

movement, influences, passions, and properties too, are communicated. So that in this hinge between two things a resemblance appears...In the vast syntax of the world, the different beings adjust themselves to one another; the plant communicates with the animal, the earth with the sea, man with everything around him. [cclxiv]

Aemulatio:

a sort of 'convenience' that has been freed from the law of place and is able to function, without motion, from a distance...There is something in emulation of the reflection and the mirror: it is the means whereby things scattered through the universe can answer one another...But the distance it crosses is not annulled by the subtle metaphor of emulation; it remains open to the eye...The links of emulation...form...a series of concentric circles reflecting and rivalling one another.[cclxv]

Analogy:

In this analogy, convenientia and aemulatio are super-imposed...it makes possible the marvelous confrontation of resemblance across space; but it also speaks...of adjacencies, of bonds and joints. Its power is immense, for the similitudes of which it treats are not the visible, substantial ones between things themselves; they need only be the more subtle resemblances of relations.[cclxvi]

Sympathies:

Sympathy plays through the depth of the universe in a free state. It can traverse the vastest spaces in an instant: it falls like a thunderbolt from the distant planet upon the man ruled by that planet...it excites the things of the world to movement and can draw even the most distant of them together. It is a principle of mobility...Sympathy is compensated for by its twin, antipathy...the sovereignty of the sympathy-antipathy pair gives rise to all the forms of resemblance.[cclxvii]

If one keeps these in mind as one reads Hume, some very interesting things begin to happen.

Hume had looked out at the world, and would see causation, would see productive power, if only he could. But he could not. There was no resemblance between causation and the precedent impressions of the world; only from observation of the mind, of the propensity of expectation, did one have such an idea. Before his very eyes the medieval world disintegrated, a million tiny drops, beads, atoms...

his face is to his body what the face of heaven is to the ether; his pulse beats in his veins as the stars circle the sky according to their own fixed paths; the seven orifices in his head are to his face what the seven planets are to the sky.[cclxviii]

The stars are the matrix of all the plants and every star in the sky is only the spiritual prefiguration of a plant, such that it represents that plant...the celestial plants and herbs are turned towards the earth and look directly down upon the plants they have procreated, imbuing them with some particular virtue.[cclxix]

Revealing great, unusual, and remarkable spectacles... above all...FOUR PLANETS swiftly revolving about Jupiter at differing distances and periods[cclxx]

In the immediate decades and centuries before Hume wrote his *Treatise,* the stars had no sooner wholly quit their divine courses and taken up mechanical orbits, they had no sooner lost their divine motive and been left gliding through the ether unattended, than a gentle force, an ordering principle, seems to begin to be seen in Hume's philosophy. Hume seemed to be asking, Where are the cords that bind the wanderers to their courses? And what binds their courses to the seasons? And the seasons to the infant, youth, woman, aged? Hume said he did not see such a cord in the world; but he did see, in the mind, in language, in words, in convention, what others before him claimed they could perceive in the world: causation. Where did he locate causation? In the human heart. The sympathies of the understanding.

If one follows Hume here, one has to ask, Were the schoolmen of the middle ages mad or liars? Did they not look into the heavens themselves? Did they not watch the billiard balls, the flame and the wax as Hume said he did, and looking, saw nothing but billiard balls, wax and flame?

> ...as a rope stretched from the first cause as far as the lowest and smallest of things, by a reciprocal and continuous connection; in such wise that the superior virtue, spreading its beams, reaches so far that if we touch one extremity of that cord it will make tremble and move all the rest.[cclxxi]

Today, reading Hume, one may ask rhetorically, What else could there be to perceive?

> When I cast my eye on the known qualities of objects...; ...the first circumstance, that strikes my eye...[cclxxii]

'But is that not what the schoolmen saw?'
'What, that

the stars…pour the whole dynasty of their influences…over the plants of the earth ?[cclxxiii]

'No, for'

when we consider these objects with the utmost attention, we find only that the one body approaches the other; and that the motion of it precedes that of the other, but without any sensible interval.[cclxxiv]

'Then what do we know?'
'That'

when any objects resemble each other, the resemblance will at first strike the eye, or rather the mind.[cclxxv]

This was Hume's skepticism and empiricism all in one breath: if it is the eye that is struck, then there is an external world; if the mind, then there is not an external world, yet there is still an impression.

'Then it is true that'

all herbs, plants, trees and other things issuing from the bowels of the earth are so many magic books and signs?[cclxxvi]

'That'

internal head ailments may be prevented by use of the nut itself 'which is exactly like the brain in appearance?[cclxxvii]

'No; just that'

all our ideas and impressions are resembling,

'and that'

habit is another principle, which determines me to expect the same for the future.[cclxxviii]

One might say that Hume shook the heavens, and demanded. He questioned, again and again. He turned them this way and that. All of nature had to give account, but she would not; she could not. She was dead, or at least dying, and no philosopher could yet revive her spirit. 'Certainty is within,' said Hume. Resemblance reigned there still. Resemblance, that gentle force, had irresistibly converged idea with impression, and human nature was born even as the heavens sighed. The Principle flickered still, and flickered bright and strong. 'It is light within,' said Hume; 'It is light within.' But without, it was night. What for the schoolmen lit the world, for Hume lit a single soul. Contiguity; convenientia. Resemblance; aemulatio.

Epilogue
Could Hume and Locke and Descartes simply not see what others before them could see? The medieval world had disappeared, certainly, but it is not clear whether that was simply due to a change in the methods of learning. Descartes can be considered as at a turning point, where the waning and waxing consciousnesses were mingled, and beginning to more profoundly separate out. Hume *did* perceive resemblance clearly enough. He did perceive principles of association. According to thinkers before him, those principles were perceived as not entirely confined to the human mind. For Hume the heavens did not reveal necessary connections, but he did find the human mind not

only to be quickened by guiding principles, gentle forces, but even more, he found the uniquely human mind, the individual mind, to *be* at all.

In the next, and last, chapter, I return to Barfield one last time.

Conclusion

Whether or not Barfield will be taken up more extensively into academic philosophy in a productive and interesting way is yet to be seen, but I hope that it has been demonstrated that his work deserves, and can bear, serious philosophical scrutiny, and will benefit from serious and imaginative development. For the time being, besides the modest effort that this book represents, there are no Barfield studies within mainstream philosophy. Only a few philosophers of all that have philosophized throughout history have become the subject of "studies." At least in terms of wealth of references to his work, Barfield is no such subject.

Why? For one, it is to be admitted that there were, and are, philosophers discussing similar notions. Kuhn's *The Structure of Scientific Revolutions*, published five years after *Saving the Appearances,* introduced the philosophically interesting notion of incommensurability, transferring it from mathematics to history of science. What was involved in the paradigm shifts in science included attention to new and/or different details of reality from the preceding paradigm. Kuhn even used the phrase "different worlds" to describe the qualitative difference between the outlook characterized by the two paradigms. Barfield showed such a shift in attention in the big picture in *Saving the Appearances,* and attributed it to the evolution of consciousness; Kuhn did not address the cause.

A search in an academic library, on the internet, or in the bookstores reveals scores of books on the topic of the evolution of consciousness.[cclxxix] These include titles like *Changes of Mind: A Holonomic Theory of the Evolution of Consciousness, Coming Into Being: Artifacts and Texts in the Evolution of Consciousness,* and *Earthbridge Crossing: A SUNY Approach to Philosophy, Quantum Physics, Spiritual Awareness, and the Evolution of Consciousness.*[cclxxx] There are conferences, websites, and degree programs that focus on the evolution of consciousness. There is no doubt that at the time he wrote *Saving the Appearances,* and even more so when he wrote *Poetic Diction,* Barfield's work was profoundly insightful. Today these concerns and conclusions are not the sole property of Owen Barfield. Yet despite this recent explosion of interest in and writing about the evolution of consciousness, the *fact* of the evolution of consciousness constitutes the basic premise of far, far fewer of the works one encounters. Most concern themselves with establishing the nature of the felt change of consciousness, whereas Barfield had already long ago begun to look into the worlds that such a change allowed.

Barfield's work is in some ways still far ahead of any work being done today. The seriousness of the last chapters of *Saving the Appearances,* and the unequivocal tenor of the conclusions regarding the origin of the earth, are not tentative conclusions, but substantive starting points for far reaching investigations. We are still left with the question why Barfield's work has not influenced philosophy in the universities.

The preceding pages were spent presenting Barfield's work in a way that he meant for it to be taken, and has not: as *bona fide* philosophical argumentation, deserving of serious discussion within mainstream philosophical boundaries. By the very act of bringing him into the philosophical fray, I hope that this objective has been at least provisionally realized. This book's investigation of Barfield's work in *Saving the Appearances* engaged classical philosophical texts, modern and contemporary issues, and basic tools of philosophical argumentation.

Now that there is at least the prima facie case for the philosophical character, and arguably the intrinsic value, of Barfield's work, I will move on, in the last remaining pages of this book, to suggest that it is only the beginnings of that work that belong to philosophy. If the conclusions reached by Barfield in *Saving the Appearances* concerning the basic facts of the evolution of consciousness are granted, one is right away in a very different place than while untangling the crumpled skein.

A familiarization with all of Barfield's work shows that though philosophy was the hammer and tongs work, the product of his labor was something quite different from, and perhaps foreign to, professional philosophy. That product was the uncovering of a spiritual landscape, a world of spiritual reality. That is what was referred to in part when he spoke of human history bathed in the light of an evolution of consciousness. Philosophy for him was apparently a chosen and enjoyable practice, but most importantly, it was a necessary one.

> A great deal of the complexity of my argument is due to the deep-seated error, with its consequently innumerable ramifications, which that argument has sought to unravel.[cclxxxi]

He took up with that task, and took up with his philosophy, with care, skill, and a sober mind. Nevertheless, for him the blessing, the reward of the sweat on his brow was the matter once it was unraveled.

> the movements of fingers disentangling a crumpled skein are complicated, but the final result is not complication.[cclxxxii]

The result in the matter of the evolution of consciousness was not only "not complication," but it was light and renewal.

The world of final participation will one day sparkle in
the light of the eye as it never yet sparkled early one morn-
ing in the original light of the sun.[cclxxxiii]

Philosophy for Barfield was that much more blessed by its service to the
unfolding of a new skein.

Though his skill and care in arguing and in treating of the history of
philosophy reveal such an attitude toward philosophy, there is other evidence of his attitude. In his autobiography *Surprised by Joy*[cclxxxiv] C.S.
Lewis spoke of Barfield's and others' role in Lewis' conversion:

Even my own pupil Griffiths—now Dom Bede
Griffiths—though not yet himself a believer, did his share.
Once, when he and Barfield were lunching in my room, I
happened to refer to philosophy as 'a subject.' 'It wasn't a
subject to Plato,' said Barfield, 'it was a way.' The quiet
but fervent agreement of Griffiths, and the quick glance of
understanding between these two, revealed to me my own
frivolity.[cclxxxv]

A friend, and now a philosophy professor, told me once that philosophy is nothing if not argument. For Barfield it was the "complicated
movements of fingers disentangling a crumpled skein." But philosophy
means, as almost every philosophy professor tells her introductory classes,
love of wisdom. This is the broader view which Barfield espoused.
Argument was for a purpose, and not an end in itself. In the Preface to the
second edition of *Poetic Diction,* Barfield took up with the arguments of
the linguistic analysis of Wittgenstein, Ayer, Ryle, and others. Twenty
years later, in the Afterword to the same book, he wrote:

The Preface to the second edition (1952) was mainly a
discussion of the opposite point of view. It was preoccupied

with those whom I will call 'enemies' for short, though I am not aware of much personal animosity.[cclxxxvi]

He then went on to say:

> When the question was raised of yet another Preface being written for this reprinting, it was decided for typographical reasons that an Afterword would be better. And I propose to use it for speaking finally, not of the 'enemies,' of whom, incidentally, I am thoroughly tired, but of 'friends' instead.[cclxxxvii]

He wrote for approximately eleven pages identifying friends to the project of elucidating moments, details, aspects, and implications of a poetic experience of language and history, of an evolution of consciousness. He mentioned and discussed Ernst Cassirer, F.M. Cornford, Bruno Snell, and Philip Wheelwright, all known and respected in philosophy. But many more he named that were not philosophers, who were outside of philosophy as a subject.

In *Miracles*[cclxxxviii] C.S. Lewis wrote what may be a helpful backdrop to Barfield's claims in the last few chapters of *Saving the Appearances* apropos of religion, because of Lewis' more traditional terminology, his relationship to Barfield, and his explicit reference to philosophers.

> The state of affairs in which ordinary people can discover the Supernatural only by abstruse reasoning is recent and, by historical standards, abnormal. All over the world, until quite modern times, the direct insight of the mystics and the reasonings of the philosophers percolated to the mass of people by authority and tradition; they could be received by those who were no great reasoners themselves in the concrete form of myth and ritual and the whole

pattern of life. In the conditions produced by a century or so of Naturalism, plain men are being forced to bear burdens which plain men were never expected to bear before. We must get to the truth ourselves or go without it.cclxxxix

Barfield's exhortation to disentangle the crumpled skein he argued was critical for religious minded folks in general, but especially so for those who called themselves Christians and who wanted to understand and obey the life and words of Christ. It appears that Barfield regarded this connection between philosophy and religion, between abstruse reasoning and the Supernatural, as essential to human health. The dawning of the light of final participation followed hard and necessarily on the heels of his work in philosophy and the history of philosophy.

The relationship between the mind and heart of man is indeed a close and delicate one and any substantial cleft between the two is unhealthy and cannot long endure.ccxc

Barfield's philosophy was not that of a dilettante, but he was interested not just in argument, but in disentangling a skein. Barfield seems, like he was said to have claimed for Plato, to have regarded philosophy not as a subject, but as a way.

There are implications and applications of Barfield's evolution of consciousness in various philosophical domains: in environmental philosophy, phenomenology, the philosophy of science, and the philosophy of language. It seems that if Barfield's work is to be of value to philosophy, though, it is his overall view, the evolution of consciousness, which will have to find its way into those fields. Then, either a discussion or refutation or embracing of religion, and maybe Christianity, is likely to follow. Perhaps this, if true, is why Barfield's work has not been taken up into mainstream philosophy. Not because that work is religious *per se*, but because in his work and thought it was the discovery of the Supernatural that was the blessing of abstruse reasoning, and not vice versa.

About the Author

Philosophy and the Evolution of Consciousness is the fruit of 13 years of study of Owen Barfield's work. Mr. Smitherman began this period with a reading of *Saving the Appearances* while teaching high school Chemistry, Physics, and Biology. He corresponded with Owen Barfield for several years, during which he took up formal graduate studies in Philosophy. He focused that study on the philosophy of language, and the philosophy of science. Mr. Smitherman is currently working on a study of Rudolf Steiner's *Philosophy of Freedom* from his home in Missoula, Montana.

Appendix

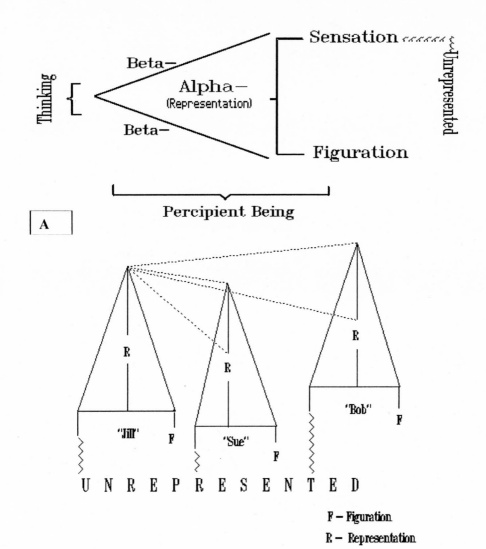

Sensation

Unrepresented

Beta—

Alpha—
(Representation)

Thinking

Beta—

Figuration

Percipient Being

A

R

R

R

"Bob"

F

"Jill"

F

"Sue"

F

U N R E P R E S E N T E D

F – Figuration

R – Representation

ORIGINAL PARTICIPATION

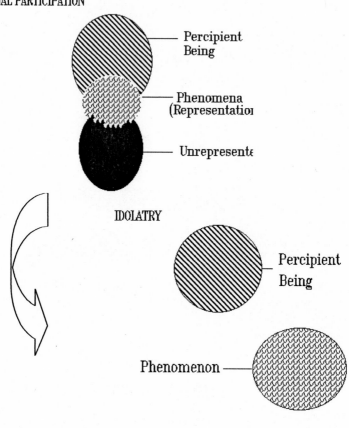

Percipient
Being

Phenomena
(Representatioi

Unrepresenta

IDOLATRY

Percipient
Being

Phenomenon

FINAL PARTICIPATION

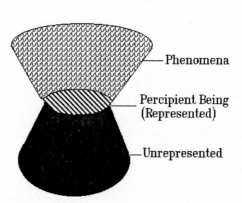

Phenomena

Percipient Being
(Represented)

Unrepresented

References

Ayer, A.J., *Language, Truth and Logic*, New York: Dover, 1952

Barfield, Owen, *History in English Words*, Hudson, NY: Lindisfarne Press, 1967

—*Poetic Diction: A Study in Meaning*, Middletown, Connecticut: Wesleyan University Press, 1973

—*Saving the Appearances: A Study in Idolatry*, New York: Harcourt, Brace & World, Inc., 1957

—*The Rediscovery of Meaning and Other Essays*, Middletown, Connecticut: Wesleyan University Press, 1977

Berman, Morris, *The Reenchantment of the World*, Ithaca: Cornell University Press, 1981

Buber, Martin, *I and Thou*, New York: Charles Scribner's Sons, 1958

Carpenter, Humphrey, ed., *The Letters of J.R.R. Tolkien*, Boston: Houghton Mifflin Company, 1981

Chicago: The University of Chicago Press, 1962.

Coleridge, Samuel Taylor, *Aids to Reflection*, Ed. H.N. Coleridge, Pickering, 1839

Copleston, Frederick, *A History of Philosophy*, New York: Image Doubleday, 1994

Crollius, O., *Traite des signatures*, Fr. trans. Lyon, 1624, in Foucault, *The Order of Things*, Random House, 1970

Davidson, Donald, "On the Very Idea of a Conceptual Scheme," Proceedings of the American Philosophical Association, 47, 1973-74
—"What Metaphors Mean," *The Philosophy of Language*, A.P. Martinich, ed., New York: Oxford University Press, 1985

Evernden, Neil, *The Social Creation of Nature*, Baltimore: The Johns Hopkins University Press, 1992

Foucault, Michel, *The Order of Things*, Random House, 1970

Galilei, Galileo, *The Starry Messenger*, Stillman Drake, trans., Anchor Books, 1957

Goodman, Nelson, *Reconceptions in Philosophy and Other Arts and Sciences*, with Catherine Z. Elgin, Indianapolis: Hackett, 1988

Hanson, N.R., *Patterns of Discovery*, Cambridge: Cambridge University Press, 1958

Hempel, Carl G., "The Empiricist Criterion of Meaning," *Revue Internationale de Philosphie*, Vol. 4, 1950

Hume, David, *A Treatise of Human Nature*, Oxford: Oxford University Press, 1989

Jones, W.T., *The Twentieth Century to Wittgenstein and Sartre*, volume V of *A History of Western Philosophy*, New York: Harcourt Brace Jovanovich, Inc., 1975

Kant, Immanuel, *Critique of Pure Reason,*Norman Kent Smith trans., 1965 edition, New York: St. Martin's Press, 1929

Lewis, C.S., *The Inspirational Writings of C.S. Lewis*, New York: Inspirational Press, 1987
—*Miracles: How God Intervenes in Nature and Human Affairs*, New York: Macmillan Publishing Company, 1960

Max Oelschlaeger, ed., *The Wilderness Condition: Essays on Environment and Civilization*, Washington, D.C.: Island Press, 1992

McDermott, Robert, "Philosophy and Evolution of Consciousness," *Cross Currents*, Vol. XXXIX, Number Three, Fall 1989

Myers, Doris, *C.S. Lewis In Context*, Kent State University Press, 1998

New York: Simon and Schuster, 1989.

Nola, Robert, ed., *Relativism and Realism in Science,* The Netherlands: Kluwer Academic Publishers, 1988

Oelschlaeger, Max, *The Idea of Wilderness: From Prehistory to the Age of Ecology,* New Haven: Yale University Press, 1991

Porta, G., *Magie Naturelle*, Fr, trans. Rouen, 1650, in Foucault, *The Order of Things*, Random House, 1970

Potts, Donna *Howard Nemerov and Objective Idealism: The Influence of Owen Barfield,* Columbia, MO: The University of Missouri Press, 1992

Rorty, Richard, *Consequences of Pragmatism,* Minneapolis: University of Minnesota Press, 1982

—"The Contingency of Language," *London Review of Books*, 17 April 1986

—"The Contingency of Selfhood," *London Review of Books*, 7 May 1986

—*Philosophy and the Mirror of Nature,* Princeton: Princeton University Press, 1979

Sartre, Jean-Paul, *Being and Nothingness: An Essay on Phenomenological Ontology,* Trans. Hazel Barnes, New York: Washington Square Press, 1966

Sessions, George, "Ecocentrism, Wilderness, and Global Ecosystem Protection," in *The Wilderness Condition: Essays on Environment and Civilization*, Ed. Max Oeschlaeger, Washington, D.C.: Island Press, 1992

Snell, Bruno, *The Discovery of the Mind: The Greek Origins of European Thought,* Cambridge: Harvard University Press, 1953

Solomon, Robert, *A History of Western Philosophy,* Oxford: Oxford University Press, 1988, Part 7, *The Rise and Fall of the Self (Continental Philosophy since 1750*

Steiner, Rudolf, *The Philosophy of Spiritual Activity [Freedom]: Fundamentals of a Modern World Conception*, Trans. Prof. and Mrs.

Hoernle, London: The Rudolf Steiner Publishing Co., 1949 (1894)

Sugerman, Shirley, ed., *Evolution of Consciousness: Studies in Polarity,* Middletown, CT: Wesleyan University Press, 1976

Suppe, Frederick, *The Structure of Scientific Theories,* Urbana: University of Illinois Press, 1977

Whitfield, Charles, *Healing the Child Within: Discovery and Recovery for Adult Children of Dysfunctional Families,* Deerfield Beach, Fla.: Health Communications, Inc.

Whorf, Benjamin, *Language, Thought and Reality,* Cambridge, Mass.: MIT Press, 1956

Index

James, William, 7, 103
Jesus, 26, 32
Jews, 31-32, 149
  Hebrew, 33
  Hebrews, 25
  israelite, 25
  Jewish, 33
Jones, 142
Jung, C.G., 2
Jupiter, 125

Kant, Immanuel, 44, 56
Kantian, 56, 60-62, 64-65, 67, 70-71, 81-82, 110
  Kantianism, 7, 70-71
Kepler, Johannes, 16
Knowledge, 9-10, 14-15, 56-58, 69-70, 74, 80-81, 98-99, 101, 104-106, 109-110, 116, 122-123
Kuhn, Thomas, 2, 17, 95, 97
  Structure of Scientific Revolutions, 2, 17, 97-98, 100, 130

Langer, Susanne, 22
Language, 26-28, 34-36, 40, 48, 54, 56, 62-67, 69-73, 93, 98-99, 108-110, 126
Latin, 123
Leibniz, 44
Levy-Bruhl, Lucien, 22
Lewis, C.S, 133
  Surprised by Joy, 4,
Lewis, C.S., 4, 133-134
Locke, John, 8, 44, 72, 116
Logic, 12, 17,
  Logical, 3, 6, 9-10, 12, 14, 73, 94, 99-100, 105, 107, 112, 118
Lord Tennyson, Alfred, 9
Lsd, 2,

Mackey, Louis, 5
Man, 11, 22, 29-31, 33, 37-38, 48-50, 76-77, 80, 124, 135

Notes

[i] Owen Barfield, *Poetic Diction: A Study in Meaning* (Middletown, Connecticut: Wesleyan University Press, 1973), 35-36.

[ii] New York: Harcourt, Brace & World, Inc..

[iii] Personal correspondence, August, 1988.

[iv] See G. B. Tennyson, "A Bibliography of the Works of Owen Barfield" in Shirley Sugerman, ed., *Evolution of Consciousness: Studies in Polarity* (Middletown, CT: Wesleyan University Press, 1976) for references in this paragraph.

[v] In *Cross Currents*, Vol. XXXIX, Number Three, Fall 1989, pp. 322-338. It might be appropriate to mention here that this article was unknown to me at the time (1992) that I completed my first draft of what is now this book, and what I then titled "Philosophy and the Evolution of Consciousness: Hope and Burden of New Sensibility."

[vi] Donna Potts, *Howard Nemerov and Objective Idealism: The Influence of Owen Barfield* (Columbia, MO: The University of Missouri Press, 1992).

[vii] For many of the details in this and the following paragraphs, see Frederick Copleston, *A History of Philosophy* (New York: Image Doubleday, 1994), especially Volume 8, *Modern Philosophy: Empiricism, Idealism and Pragmatism in Britain and the United States*.

[viii] In *C.S. Lewis In Context* (Kent State University Press, 1998). I want to acknowledge my debt to Doris Myers for showing me the value of placing Barfield in the context of the philosophical issues that surrounded him in the beginning years of the development of his philosophy. I also want to acknowledge my debt to her for the title of this chapter.

[ix] Copleston, *A History,* Volume 8, 262.

[x] David Hume, *A Treatise of Human Nature,* (Oxford: Oxford University Press, 1989), 4.

[xi] Hume, *A Treatise,* 4.

[xii] Hume, *A Treatise,* 647-648.

[xiii] Hume, *A Treatise,* 647-648.

[xiv] Hume, *A Treatise,* 104.

[xv] *The Twentieth Century to Wittgenstein and Sartre,* volume V of *A History of Western Philosophy,* W.T. Jones (New York: Harcourt Brace Jovanovich, Inc., 1975), 218.

[xvi] Jones, 219.

[xvii] Jones, 156.

[xviii] Owen Barfield, *Poetic Diction: A Study in Meaning* (Middletown, Connecticut: Wesleyan University Press, 1973)

[xix] Barfield, *Poetic Diction,* 129.

[xx] Owen Barfield's *History in English Words* (Hudson, NY: Lindisfarne Press, 1967) demonstrates this wonderfully. But even the dictionary shows many such words, even very recent ones. For instance, a century ago the word "addict" had only a verbal form, meaning to be held or bound to. Its connotations were as positive then as today they are negative. So one could be "addicted to the study of Scripture."

[xxi] Barfield, 102-103.

[xxii] Barfield, 61, emphasis added.

[xxiii] Barfield, 85.

[xxiv] Carl G. Hempel, "The Empiricist Criterion of Meaning," *Revue Internationale de Philosphie,* Vol. 4, 1950.

[xxv] Hempel, "The Empiricist Criterion of Meaning."

[xxvi] Hempel, "The Empiricist Criterion of Meaning."

[xxvii] A.J. Ayer, *Language, Truth and Logic* (New York: Dover, 1952), 36.

[xxviii] Ayer, *Language, Truth and Logic,* 36.

xxix Ayer, *Language, Truth and Logic*, 36.

xxx Ayer, *Language, Truth and Logic*, 36.

xxxi N. R. Hanson, *Patterns of Discovery,* (Cambridge: Cambridge University Press, 1958), 5.

xxxii Hanson, *Discovery,* 5.

xxxiii Owen Barfield, *Saving the Appearances: A Study in Idolatry* (New York, 1957). Hereafter *SA*. A later edition is published by Wesleyan University Press, Middletown, Conn., 1988.

xxxiv Psalm 115, quoted in Barfield, *SA*, 111

xxxv Barfield, *SA*, 124.

xxxvi Barfield, *SA*, 42.

xxxvii Barfield, *SA,* 12

xxxviii Barfield, *SA,* 17

xxxix Barfield, *SA*, 21. See the Appendix, Diagram 1.A., for this term, as well as terms to follow. See the Appendix, Diagram B for a schematic representation of the collective aspect of "collective representations." It shows the connection between the alpha- and beta-thinking of several individuals. Specifically, it shows the beta-thinking of "Jill," in relation to the alpha- and beta-thinking of "Sue" and "Bob." The dotted lines indicate mostly verbal communication, but also could include artistic expression. Notice that each of these person's structure is the same as the structure of sketch A.

xl Barfield, *SA*, p. 18.

xli Barfield, *SA*, p. 22.

xlii Barfield, *SA*, p. 23.

xliii One can imagine introducing coffee to someone who has never smelled nor heard of coffee. They will not only not have the word "coffee," but they will not have knowledge of coffee. This illustration points out at the least that sensation and figuration are distinct.

xliv Barfield, *SA*, 24. See the Appendix, Diagram A.

xlv Barfield, *SA*, 24.

xlvi Barfield, *SA*, 25. See the Appendix, Diagram A.

xlvii Barfield, *SA*, 24. See the Appendix, Diagram B.

xlviii Barfield, *SA*, 25.

xlix Barfield, *SA*, 35.

l Barfield, *SA*, 24.

li See Barfield, *SA*, 26-27.

lii Barfield makes it clear that the anthropology of his day is taken up in order to illustrate, not in order to prove. It is meant to give the reader an idea of what he means by participation, and not to prove that in fact participation is real. For proof he takes the etymological approach. That is the substance of later parts of this book. For the sake of his argument, distinction between anthropology and physical science as sciences is denied; there is only one science: that which tells us what the world is really like. Historically speaking, anthropology, like all the other sciences, worked hard to emulate physical science in method, and in actual doctrines.

liii Barfield, *SA*, 28.

liv Barfield, *SA*, 33.

lv Barfield, *SA*, 28.

lvi Barfield, *SA*, 40.

lvii Bruno Snell, in his book *The Discovery of the Mind: The Greek Origins of European Thought* (Cambridge: Harvard University Press, 1953) is instructive here, and is discussed at length in a later chapter. Apropos of Homer's worldview, and the difference of that worldview from even the classical Greek worldview, Snell says that difference "can be shown from his language." [p. 1] Snell realizes that his approach takes it for granted "that if [the authors of ancient texts] were cognizant of a thing they said so." [p. 311, note #3] He adds that "this may not be convincing in all cases...but for our present purposes it must suffice." [p. 311, note #3] This too seems to be Barfield's method. To respond to the question, "Why must this suffice?" the answer is simply, "How else would we go about such a study?" If the objection is then raised, in the form of a rhetorical question, "Yes, indeed, how else?" implying that such a study can only be a fruitless conundrum, the response is the work itself. Whether it is fruitful or not must wait until the end.

lviii Barfield, *SA*, 40. See the Appendix, Diagram C.

[lix] Lucien Levy-Bruhl, *How Natives Think*, in Barfield, *SA*, 29.

[lx] Levy-Bruhl, in Barfield, *SA*, 29-30.

[lxi] Levy-Bruhl, in Barfield, *SA*, 30.

[lxii] Barfield, *SA*, 31, 34.

[lxiii] Barfield, *SA*, 34.

[lxiv] Barfield, *SA*, 42.

[lxv] Barfield, *SA*, 24.

[lxvi] Barfield, *SA*, 41.

[lxvii] Barfield, *SA*, 34.

[lxviii] This last text is included, even though it is not an ancient text, because it clearly illustrates Barfield's point, and because the author presented that text as having been written by an author of a different world. Tolkien spent his life studying the Norse sagas and other of the oldest European texts, and his Trilogy was intended to read just as those texts do; it was meant to be English myth which Tolkien saw that England lacked. Further, Tolkien was familiar with Barfield's work, at the very least with *Poetic Diction*. See *The Letters of J.R.R. Tolkien*, ed. Humphrey Carpenter, Boston: Houghton Mifflin Company, 1981, p22.

[lxix] It may be argued that authentic originally participatory texts are simply the work of anthropomorphism. But "anthropomorphism" in this context begs the question, at least in regard to the most ancient texts, for in those texts "human" and "non-human" are not mutually exclusive, and sometimes not very distinct, classes—which is the necessary and fundamental assumption underlying the notion of anthropomorphism.

[lxx] *Time*, December 4, 1989, pp. 11-13.

[lxxi] See note 20 above.

[lxxii] Barfield, *SA*, 42.

[lxxiii] Barfield, *SA*, 42.

[lxxiv] Barfield, *Poetic Diction*, 79.

[lxxv] Barfield, *Poetic Diction*, 79.

[lxxvi] Barfield, *Poetic Diction*, 79, 80-81.

lxxvii Barfield, *Poetic Diction*, 85.

lxxviii Barfield, *SA*, 44.

lxxix Barfield, *SA*, 44.

lxxx Barfield, *SA*, 45.

lxxxi Barfield, *SA*, 66.

lxxxii Barfield, *SA*, 43.

lxxxiii See the Appendix, Diagram D.

lxxxiv Barfield, *SA*, 53.

lxxxv Barfield, *SA*, 50.

lxxxvi Barfield, *SA*, 51.

lxxxvii Barfield, *SA*, 51.

lxxxviii Barfield, *SA*, 52.

lxxxix Barfield, *SA*, 39.

xc Barfield, *SA*, 65-66.

xci Psalm 115, in Barfield, *SA*, 111.

xcii Barfield suggests that this impulse on the part of the Jews to refrain from fixing on the appearances as a place of abode of the 'other' indicates an inevitability of the progression from original participation to idolatry. "This tendency [to abstract the sense-content from the whole representation and seek that for its own sake, transmuting the admired image into a desired object] seems always to have been latent in original participation." (Barfield, *SA*, 111)

xciii Barfield, *SA*, 114.

xciv Barfield, *SA*, 114.

xcv Barfield, *SA*, 182. The Divine Name: the "I AM," the Word, the Logos, the Creative Principle.

xcvi Barfield, *SA*, 144.

xcvii Barfield, *SA*, 129. See the Appendix, Diagram E.

xcviii Barfield, *SA*, 132.

xcix Barfield, *SA*, 137.

[c] Barfield, *SA*, 132.

[ci] Barfield, *SA*, 132.

[cii] Barfield, *SA*, 160.

[ciii] Barfield, *SA*, 65 and passim.

[civ] Barfield, *SA*, 116.

[cv] Owen Barfield, *History in English Words* (New York: George H. Doran, 1926); *Poetic Diction: A Study in Meaning* (1928, 1952. New York: McGraw-Hill, 1964). *Poetic Diction* is now published by Wesleyan University Press, Middletown, Conn., 1973, and is in its third edition.

[cvi] Barfield, *SA*, 142.

[cvii] Barfield, *SA*.

[cviii] Barfield, *SA*, 142.

[cix] Barfield, *SA*, 72.

[cx] Barfield, *SA*, 72.

[cxi] Barfield, *SA*, 73.

[cxii] Barfield, *SA*, 74.

[cxiii] Barfield, *SA*, 74.

[cxiv] If meaning is taken as the relation between thoughts and things, then created meaning is a relation wrought by deliberate imaginal effort, as in poetic metaphor. The important point to remember about original participation is that it was an immediate—a perceptual—experience of meaning, as opposed to a merely conceptual relation.

[cxv] Barfield, *Poetic Diction*, 102 and passim; *SA*, Chapter XIX.

[cxvi] Barfield, *SA*, 130.

[cxvii] Barfield, *SA*, 131.

[cxviii] Barfield, *SA*, 132.

[cxix] Barfield, *SA*, 132.

[cxx] Barfield, 23.

[cxxi] Barfield, 53.

[cxxii] Owen Barfield, *The Rediscovery of Meaning and Other Essays* (Middletown,

Connecticut: Wesleyan University Press, 1977), 215.

cxxiii Barfield, "Science and Quality," *The Rediscovery of Meaning*, 176.

cxxiv Barfield, "Science and Quality," 176.

cxxv Barfield, *Saving the Appearances*, 61.

cxxvi Barfield, *Saving the Appearances*, 63.

cxxvii Barfield, *Saving the Appearances*, 66.

cxxviii Barfield, *Saving the Appearances*, 66.

cxxix Norman Kent Smith trans., 1965 edition (New York: St. Martin's Press, 1929).

cxxx Kant, *Critique*, 112.

cxxxi Kant, Critique, 111.

cxxxii Kant, Critique, 112.

cxxxiii Kant, *Critique*, 268.

cxxxiv Kant, *Critique*, 268.

cxxxv Robert Solomon's book on continental philosophy is subtitled *The Rise and Fall of the Self* (*Continental Philosophy since 1750*, Part 7 of *A History of Western Philosophy* [Oxford: Oxford University Press, 1988]), and begins with the time of Kant.

cxxxvi Richard Rorty, "The World Well Lost," *Consequences of Pragmatism* (Minneapolis: University of Minnesota Press, 1982), 3.

cxxxvii Rorty, "World," 3.

cxxxviii Rorty, "World," 4.

cxxxix Rorty, "World," 4.

cxl See Donald Davidson's "On the Very Idea of a Conceptual Scheme," Proceedings of the American Philosophical Association, 47, 1973-74.

cxli Rorty, "World," 17.

cxlii Rorty, "World," 15.

cxliii Rorty, "World," 17.

cxliv Rorty, "World," 16.

cxlv Richard Rorty, "The Contingency of Language," *London Review of Books*, 17 April 1986; and "The Contingency of Selfhood," *London Review of Books*, 7 May 1986.

cxlvi Rorty, "World," 16.

cxlvii Rorty, "Language," 6.

cxlviii Rorty, "Language," 3.

cxlix Rorty, "Language," 3.

cl Rorty, "Language, 6.

cli Rorty, "Self," 11.

clii Rorty, "Self," 12.

cliii Rorty, "Self," 14.

cliv Rorty, "Self," 14.

clv Barfield, *SA*, 134.

clvi Barfield, *SA*, 129.

clvii Donald Davidson, "What Metaphors Mean," *The Philosophy of Language*, A.P. Martinich, ed. (New York: Oxford University Press, 1985).

clviii Owen Barfield, "Poetic Diction and Legal Fiction," *The Rediscovery of Meaning, and Other Essays* (Middletown, Conn.: Wesleyan University Press, 1977).

clix As in Davidson, "Metaphors," 447.

clx Barfield, *Poetic Diction*, 48.

clxi Barfield, *Saving the Appearances*, 64

clxii See Morris Berman, *The Reenchantment of the World* (Ithaca: Cornell University Press, 1981), Chapter 5. There Berman argues that the physical human body, as westerners experience it, is now the evolutionary analog, the evolved form, of Kant's *ding-an-sich*, in that the body for us today and the *ding-an-sich* have common characteristics.

clxiii Jean-Paul Sartre, Being and Nothingness: An Essay on Phenomenological Ontology. Trans. Hazel Barnes. New York: Washington Square Press, 1966.

clxiv Sartre, 267-8.

clxv Sartre, 308.

clxvi Sartre, 309.

clxvii Sartre, 311.

clxviii Sartre, 311.

clxix Sartre, 311.

clxx Sartre, 311.

clxxi Sartre, 311.

clxxii Sartre, 311-13.

clxxiii Sartre, 315. I am not convinced that this unique phenomenon suggests itself as probably a man, insofar as it is entirely phenomenal, because what we want is a for-itself, not a unique phenomenon. So why the 'hunch' at all?

clxxiv Sartre, 315.

clxxv Sartre, 317. I will argue later on that this experience is indistinguishable from our own experience of the for-itself.

clxxvi Sartre, 317.

clxxvii Sartre, 317.

clxxviii Sartre, 317.

clxxix Sartre, 319.

clxxx Sartre, 525.

clxxxi Rudolf Steiner, The Philosophy of Spiritual Activity [Freedom]: Fundamentals of a Modern World Conception. Trans. Prof. and Mrs. Hoernle. London: The Rudolf Steiner Publishing Co., 1949 (1894). xiii.

clxxxii Steiner, 218.

clxxxiii Steiner, xiv.

clxxxiv Steiner, 6.

clxxxv Steiner, 9.

clxxxvi Steiner, 9.

clxxxvii Steiner, 10.

clxxxviii Steiner, 19.

clxxxix Steiner, 211.

[cxc] Steiner, 211.

[cxci] Steiner, 213.

[cxcii] Steiner, 212.

[cxciii] Steiner, 67.

[cxciv] Steiner, 212.

[cxcv] Steiner, 41.

[cxcvi] Steiner, 37.

[cxcvii] Steiner, 85.

[cxcviii] Steiner, 66-7.

[cxcix] Steiner, 64.

[cc] Steiner, 113.

[cci] Steiner, 212-13.

[ccii] Sartre, 312.

[cciii] Samuel Taylor Coleridge, Aids to Reflection, Ed. H.N. Coleridge. Pickering, 1839. 17. Cited in Owen Barfield, What Coleridge Thought, Middletown, Conn.: Wesleyan University Press, 1971. 19.

[cciv] Charles Whitfield, Healing the Child Within: Discovery and Recovery for Adult Children of Dysfunctional Families. Deerfield Beach, Fla.: Health Communications, Inc., 1987. 11.

[ccv] S. Smalley, cited in S. Wegscheider-Cruse. Cited in Whitfield, 29.

[ccvi] Subby, 1984. Cited in Whitfield, 29. Owen Barfield in various places speaks of the 'rules' of contemporary thought—idolatry—that imprison us in our bodies of skin and bone, without any meaning.

[ccvii] A.W. Schaef, Co-Dependence: Misdiagnosed and Mistreated. Cited in Whitfield, 29.

[ccviii] S. Smalley. Cited in Wegscheider-Cruse. Cited in Whitfield, 29.

[ccix] Whitfield, 29.

[ccx] Whitfield, 49.

[ccxi] Whitfield, 44.

[ccxii] Whitfield, 48.

ccxiii Whitfield, 48.

ccxiv Whitfield, 49.

ccxv I don't think it would make much sense to understand the term "psychological" in Whitfield's text to mean "in distinction from ontological."

ccxvi See also Martin Buber, *I and Thou* (New York: Charles Scribner's Sons, 1958), second edition, Postscript, sections 2, 3, and 4, whose discussions here helped me greatly to articulate my own experiences.

ccxvii Satre, 317.

ccxviii George Sessions, "Ecocentrism, Wilderness, and Global Ecosystem Protection," in The Wilderness Condition: Essays on Environment and Civilization. Ed. Max Oeschlaeger. Washington, D.C.: Island Press, 1992. 130.

ccxix Whitfield, 127.

ccxx Whitfield, 127.

ccxxi Chicago: The University of Chicago Press, 1962.

ccxxii Richard Rorty's *Philosophy and the Mirror of Nature* (Princeton: Princeton University Press, 1979) recast the history of philosophy since Kant (but really, since the beginning) in a way very disturbing to many philosophers, and acknowledges both Feyerabend and Kuhn as fellow laborers in that project of recasting.

ccxxiii Kuhn, 4.

ccxxiv Feyerabend, 175-6.

ccxxv New York: Simon and Schuster, 1989.

ccxxvi Berman, *Senses,* 297.

ccxxvii Cambridge: Harvard University Press, 1953. Trans. T. G. Rosenmeyer.

ccxxviii Max Oelschlaeger's *The Idea of Wilderness: From Prehistory to the Age of Ecology* (New Haven: Yale University Press, 1991), Neil Evernden's *The Social Creation of Nature* (Baltimore: The Johns Hopkins University Press, 1992), Paul Shepard's "A Post-Historic Primitivism," George Sessions' "Ecocentrism, Wilderness, and Global Ecosystem Protection," and Michael Zimmerman's "The Blessing of Otherness: Wilderness and the Human Condition" (all in *The Wilderness Condition: Essays on Environment and Civilization,* Max Oelschlaeger, ed., Washington, D.C.: Island Press, 1992) come to mind.

ccxxix Kuhn, *Structure*, vi.

ccxxx Benjamin Whorf, *Language, Thought and Reality,* (Cambridge, Mass.: MIT Press, 1956), 218.

ccxxxi Kuhn, *Structure*, 4.

ccxxxii Frederick Suppe, *The Structure of Scientific Theories,* (Urbana: University of Illinois Press, 1977), 2nd edition.

ccxxxiii See Suppe, 150-151.

ccxxxiv Dating conservatively from the publication of the collection of essays, *Relativism and Realism in Science,* Robert Nola, ed. (The Netherlands: Kluwer Academic Publishers, 1988).

ccxxxv Kuhn, *Structure*, 122.

ccxxxvi As in Kuhn, *Structure*, 113.

ccxxxvii Kuhn, *Structure*, 111.

ccxxxviii Kuhn, *Structure*, 129.

ccxxxix Suppe, 636-637.

ccxl Feyerabend makes clear that 'anything goes' is to be understood from the traditional view, since according to this view only a very narrow conception of rationality is operative, and it is according to and within this rationality that progress and science are to be judged and understood.

ccxli Feyerabend, *Method*, 267.

ccxlii Suppe, *Theories*, 644.

ccxliii Kuhn, "Second Thoughts on Paradigms," in The *Structure* of Scientific Theories, 463.

ccxliv Suppe, *Theories*, 138.

ccxlv It seems that I remember a rather enlightening discussion of this phenomenon of 'pattern within pattern', in the context of music and musical "themes" in Nelson Goodman's *Reconceptions in Philosophy and Other Arts and Sciences,* with Catherine Z. Elgin (Indianapolis: Hackett, 1988).

ccxlvi Feyerabend, Method, 260.

ccxlvii Snell, xi.

ccxlviii Snell, xiii

ccxlix Snell, xiii.

ccl Feyerabend, 261.

ccli This way of putting it might be sufficient as the recognition of potentially radically different interpretations, differences that make all the difference in the world. But because one lives in a world of science, the range for interpretations is extremely small: one can only make radical scientific (philosophers read 'rational') claims, one cannot make non-scientific claims.

cclii Feyerabend, 219.

ccliii Throughout I use "perception" in its broadest sense, for the very reason that otherwise one is tempted to reduce everything back down to material objectivity and objects. That is a difficult task, though; the book in its entirety is meant as an attempt to avoid such reductive relapse.

ccliv With meditation, to the degree that one participates in it, one begins to apprehend the body in a way that can only bring this fact out in a dramatic way.

cclv Berman, 297.

cclvi See Steven Weinberg, "Reflections of a Working Scientist," 44, in his comment about the dangers of the subjectivity of "gurus and flower-children."

cclvii In "Observation Reconsidered" (*Philosophy of Science 51:* 23-Jerry Fodor says, "there is nothing that nouns sound like, nothing that they look like on an oscilloscope." So also there is nothing that a quark "looks like" at the subconscious level, nor a dream-dog in waking life.

cclviii Barfield, *Saving the Appearances,* 75-76.

cclix "On the connection of ideas," *Language, Thought, and Reality: Selected Writings of Benjamin Lee Whorf,* John B. Carroll ed. (Cambridge, Mass.: MIT Press), 1956.

cclx Whorf, 35.

cclxi Whorf, 35.

cclxii Is this circular reasoning, that the definiteness of the phenomena is evident in the definiteness of descriptions of experiments meant to demonstrate that very phenomena? In other words, how do we know that the experiment did in fact demonstrate that phenomena? It seems to me that that is exactly the tale to be told here: How an idea might appear, if it could.

cclxiii Whorf, 38. Emphasis added.

cclxiv Michel Foucault, *The Order of Things*, (Random House, 1970), p. 18.

cclxv Foucault, pp. 19, 21.

cclxvi Foucault, p. 21.

cclxvii Foucault, pp. 23, 24, 25.

cclxviii O. Crollius, *Traite des signatures*, Fr. trans. Lyon, 1624, p. 88, in Foucault, p. 22.

cclxix Crollius, p. 18, in Foucault, p. 20.

cclxx Galileo Galilei, *The Starry Messenger*, title page, trans. by Stillman Drake, Anchor Books, 1957.

cclxxi G. Porta, *Magie Naturelle*, Fr, trans. Rouen, 1650, 22, in Foucault, 19.

cclxxii David Hume, *A Treatise of Human Nature*, P.H. Nidditch ed., Oxford, 1989, 77, 2.

cclxxiii Foucault, p. 20.

cclxxiv Hume, p. 77.

cclxxv Hume, p. 70.

cclxxvi Crollius, p. 6, in Foucault, p. 27.

cclxxvii Crollius, p. 33-4, in Foucault, p. 27.

cclxxviii Hume, pp. 3, 265.

cclxxix At a bookseller's web site, a search produced 90 titles for the keywords "evolution of consciousness", though approximately half of those are now out of print. The keywords "philosophy and the evolution of consciousness" returned 29 titles. At another site, the keywords "philosophy and evolution" returned 605 titles! "Philosophy and evolution of consciousness" returned 29 titles.

cclxxx Respectively: Jenny Wade, 1996; William Irwin Thompson, 1996; Sydne Heather Schinkel and Thomas Schinkel.

cclxxxi Barfield, *Saving the Appearances*, 163.

cclxxxii Barfield, *Saving the Appearances*, 163.

cclxxxiii Barfield, *Saving the Appearances*, 161.

cclxxxiv As in *The Inspirational Writings of C.S. Lewis* (New York: Inspirational Press, 1987).

cclxxxv Lewis, *Surprised by Joy,* 123.

cclxxxvi Barfield, *Poetic Diction,* 212.

cclxxxvii Barfield, *Poetic Diction,* 214.

cclxxxviii *Miracles: How God Intervenes in Nature and Human Affairs* (New York: Macmillan Publishing Company, 1960).

cclxxxix Lewis, *Miracles,* 42.

ccxc Barfield, *Saving the Appearances,* 164.